Randolph County:
A Brief History

Finished Feb 6, 2015

Randolph County:
A Brief History

Slaves 6, 50, 43, 33, 53,
Relocate to Indiana & Ohio 16, 39, 40, 43, 50, 56, 65

underground Railroad 54, 43,

saltworks 55,
Anti-Saloon League 82
Rosenwald 89
C. A. Barnett, A. A. edire. 112-3

L. Barron Mills Jr.

Office of Archives and History
North Carolina Department of Cultural Resources
Raleigh
2008

Printed by Edwards Brothers Inc.

Contents

Illustrations and Tables vii

Foreword ix

1. From Origins to Revolution 1

2. Independence and a New County Established 22

3. Communities, Leaders, and Civil War 38

4. From Reconstruction to the Close of the
   Nineteenth Century 66

5. Randolph from 1900 to 1945 87

6. Ushering in a New Millennium 105

7. Epilogue 124

Works Consulted 139

Index 143

Illustrations and Tables

Bishop August Gottlieb Spangenberg 5
Sandy Creek Baptist Church 10
Back Creek Friends Meeting 11
Edmund Fanning 13
Plaque at Alamance Battleground State Historic Site 15
Lord Charles Cornwallis. 19
Walker's Mill 20
Marker for Martha MacFarlane McGee Bell. 21
Andrew Jackson. 24
Sapona Cotton Mill (previously Cedar Falls Manufacturing
 Company) and Cedar Falls Covered Bridge 27
Mill houses at Sapona Cotton Mill 28
Train schedule for the North Carolina Railroad
 (May 15, 1881) 30
Plank road 31
Asheborough Female Academy (pre-restoration) 36
Asheborough Female Academy (post-restoration) 37
Allen U. Tomlinson 38
Trinity College (1891) 40
Gov. Jonathan Worth 44
Five daughters of Gov. Jonathan Worth 45
James Madison Leach 48
Reverend Braxton Craven 52
Thomas and Mary Hinshaw 57
The Trinity Guard. 59
Gen. George Stoneman 63
Minié balls found at Bethel Methodist Protestant Church . . 64
Gov. Jonathan Worth tombstone 67
Yow's Mill 72
Picnickers at Naomi Falls Dam (1910) 73
Naomi Wise tombstone 73

Randolph County Courthouse (1835-1909) 75
Depot Street (now Sunset Avenue) in downtown
    Asheboro 77
Map of Randolph County drawn by J. W. Bean (1873) . . 81
Memorial Hospital in Asheboro 82
Pisgah Covered Bridge 85
Swan[n]anoa Street in downtown Liberty 88
Millworkers at Acme-McCrary Corporation mill 90
Company K soldiers at Camp Sevier,
    South Carolina (ca. 1917) 92
Capt. Ben F. Dixon 93
Pottery made by Ben W. Owen 96
President John F. Kennedy seated in a "Carolina Rocker" . . 98
P&P Chair Company in Asheboro 99
Laura Stimson Worth 101
Gasoline ration book from World War II 104
Ivey B. Luck 108
Dr. Henry Jordan 110
George Washington Carver College (1954) 113
Randolph Fall Festival contest winners (1976) 116
Dorothy Cole Auman 117
Gazelles at the North Carolina Zoo 120
Construction of artificial rocks at the North Carolina Zoo . 121
Table of Randolph County Crop Statistics (2005) 125
Table of Randolph County Livestock Statistics (2005) . . . 125
New Randolph County Courthouse (2002) 129
Pavilion area at the North Carolina Zoo 132
Pisgah Covered Bridge washed away by rainwater (2003) . 133
Richard Petty (1994) 134
Shoppers at the North Carolina Pottery Center (1998) . . 136
Avery Owen, Ben Owen III, and
    LoriAnn Little Owen (2002) 137

Foreword

With the publication of *Randolph County: A Brief History*, the Historical Publications Section has now issued fifteen brief county histories. (Lenoir and Rowan are currently out of print but plans include updating and indexing them for future publication.) The section began publishing the county history series in 1963. Over the years students, teachers, tourists, scholars, and genealogists have come to rely on the county histories for their research needs. The brief histories offer pertinent data, broad surveys, and sound interpretations of people, places, and regions that have enriched North Carolina's diverse heritage.

The author of *Randolph County: A Brief History* is Lapsley Barron Mills Jr. He was born July 17, 1927 in Mooresville, which is located in Iredell County. Mills graduated from the University of North Carolina at Chapel Hill in 1949 with an A.B. in journalism. He then served as editor of the *Alamance News* in Graham; as bureau manager for United Press in Memphis, Tennessee and Charlotte; and as department editor of the *Winston-Salem Journal*. A resident of Randolph County since March 1955, Mills served as editor and publisher of the *Randolph Guide* until 1991. He has been a member of the Randolph County Historical Society since 1956 and currently holds the positions of director and secretary.

Walt Evans, former editor with the section, began the project and Denise Craig, his successor, has seen it to fruition by editing the text, selecting pertinent images, and preparing the index. Susan Trimble typeset the manuscript and designed the cover.

Donna E. Kelly, *Administrator*
Historical Publications Section

Randolph County

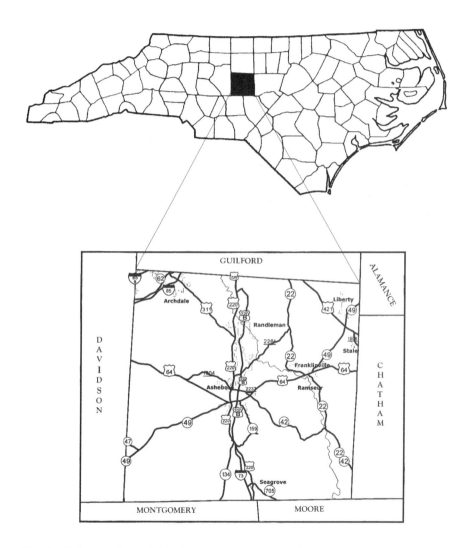

This detailed map of Randolph County shows major highways as they existed in 2006. Prepared by the Geographic Information Systems Office of the Department of Transportation.

CHAPTER ONE

From Origins to Revolution

---•+━◆━+•---

*L*ocated in the geographical center of North Carolina, in the state's Piedmont region, Randolph County is an almost perfectly square parcel of land in the Carolina slate belt. Rock formations lie close to the surface in much of the area, with volcanic rock and quartz deposits estimated to be ten to fifteen thousand feet deep. Randolph encompasses 789 square miles and is the eleventh largest county in the state.

A unique feature of Randolph County is its two distinct natural drainage systems, created by numerous creeks and branches and three rather large rivers: Deep River, Uwharrie River, and Little River. Deep River becomes a part of the Cape Fear River system, which flows into the ocean at Wilmington, North Carolina. The Uwharrie (Uharrie) River joins the Yadkin to form the Pee Dee River, and Little River merges into the Pee Dee farther south. The Pee Dee then enters South Carolina (where it is often called the Great Pee Dee) and flows into Winyah Bay near Georgetown.

The area's climate is temperate, with an average annual temperature of 60 degrees, factoring in a mean of 42 degrees in January and 75 in June. The average annual precipitation measures 45 inches (plus 7 inches of snowfall), and usually there are in excess of 200 frost-free days. The forests contain second-growth pines and hardwoods. Of the forty-six thousand acres of woodlands held within the Uwharrie National Forest, ten thousand are situated in Randolph County. Known as the Uwharrie Reservation when it was purchased by the federal government in 1931, and declared a national forest by John F. Kennedy in 1961, Uwharrie National Forest is one of four national forests in the state and the only one in the Piedmont. The other three are Croatan, Nantahala, and Pisgah National Forests.

The county's soil ranges in type from the rich loam of the creek and river bottoms to the hues of red clay found in most farmlands, with pockets of yellow clays and sandy loam. Within Randolph County is a wide variety of minerals, but their insufficient quantities historically have made mining a cost-prohibitive venture. Pyrophyllite (a silicate resembling talc, used for ceramic wares), quartz, iron, and copper have been mined in limited quantities, and in the nineteenth century gold attracted much attention. At one time there were more than fifty active gold mines, all later abandoned.

The county's lowest points of elevation lie approximately four hundred feet above sea level. Dominating the landscape are the Uwharrie Mountains, which cover nearly half of the county. This range extends eastward on an inclined plane, and the southern portion declines in elevation more than six hundred feet from west to east. Geologists believe these peaks were once quite lofty, but not as high as North Carolina's Blue Ridge Mountains, which have an average elevation of roughly three thousand feet. The Uwharries' highest peak, Shepherd Mountain, rises to only 1,390 feet. Geologists believe these mountains are the oldest range east of the Mississippi River; they were formed by volcanic activity and later eroded.

To swap blankets and trinkets with the indigenous inhabitants, many traders came into the area prior to 1674 traveling on existing trails that crossed paths in the county. Animals created the trails by cutting through woodlands to reach watering holes and grazing land, and the Native Americans followed these paths. The most highly traveled one was the Great Trading Path (also known as Occaneechi Trail and translated as "where people gather"), which originated in the vicinity of modern-day Petersburg, Virginia. The Great Trading Path followed a southwesterly route, entering present-day Randolph County at Julian and passing near the intersection of U.S. 311 and U.S. 220 business highways south of Randleman. It then crossed South Carolina and terminated near Augusta, Georgia. A lesser American Indian trading path that coursed through Randolph originated at Cross Creek (now Fayetteville, North Carolina) on the much-traveled Cape Fear River and led to the Blue Ridge Mountains. (In 1733 Edward Moseley, surveyor to the king of England, drew a map depicting the territory lying between North Carolina's Coastal Plain and the Yadkin River, showing five sites and features of this area: "the Indian Trading Path, the Keeauwee Old Town, Totero Fort, Uhwarre River, and Deep River.")

In 1670 John Lederer, a German-born trader from Petersburg, Virginia, led an exploration party through the North Carolina Piedmont, traveling as far west as the Catawba River. Lederer provided accounts of the "Wateree Indians" of the Randolph County area. The actual location of their village has not been determined. However, many generic Indian relics and artifacts have been found in an area about eight miles northwest of Asheboro, near Caraway Creek, and a large stone oven believed to have been used by the Indians still stands about three miles south of the town of Ramseur. Later, in 1694, John Needham and Gabriel Arthur, traders employed by Abraham Wood of Fort Henry, Virginia, passed through the area to trade with the Catawba Indians.

John Lawson, surveyor-general of North Carolina, related the most extensive accounts of the area's Native Americans. Lawson made a thousand-mile trek across the state and recorded his findings in his book, *A New Voyage to Carolina*, published in London in 1709. An entry for February 3, 1701, reads:

Five Miles from this River [Lawson spelled it "Heighwaree"] to the N. W. stands the Keyauwees town. They are fortified in with wooden Puncheons [sharpened wood sticks to keep others out], like Saponi [an Indian tribe], being a People of much the same Number. Nature has so fortified this Town with Mountains, that were it in a Seat of War, it might easily be made impregnable; having large Corn Fields joining to their Cabins, and a Savanna near the Town, at the Foot of these Mountains, that is capable of keeping some hundred of Heads of Cattle. And all this environed round with very high Mountains, so that no hard Wind ever troubles these Inhabitants.

Lawson reported that the Keyauwees routinely ate deer, turkey, raccoon, beaver, and bear, as well as fish and mollusks. The men hunted; the women planted corn, beans, and squash, and harvested berries, persimmons, plums, and grain from the wild. Like the Sioux, the Keyauwees made their homes with circles of poles set in the ground and tied together at the top to make a domed framework. They covered these structures with bark tied to the poles. Houses stood grouped together in stockades.

Lawson and two fellow travelers feasted with Keyauwee Jack, husband of the queen, in a cave Lawson described as spacious enough to comfortably seat one hundred men. Generations of adventurers, intrigued by Lawson's account, have unsuccessfully sought the location of this cave. Most of the searches have centered on the Ridges Mountain vicinity, an area in the Uwharries where huge boulders dominate the landscape. Adding to the mystique is Lawson's description of an Indian princess whom he regarded as the "beautifulest Indian" he ever saw.

The location of the Keyauwee village remained a puzzle until the late 1920s, when Dr. Douglas Rights of Winston-Salem, an archaeologist and minister, found the lost village and uncovered artifacts including projectile points, axes, bird-bone beads, shell beads, and clay pottery. In 1939, archaeologist Dr. Joffre Coe of Greensboro undertook a more extensive excavation. One burial mound, similar to the one excavated and restored at Town Creek in Montgomery County, North Carolina, still remains, not far from the site of the Keyauwee village.

The intriguing story of American Indians who inhabited Randolph County is revisited in two books on North Carolina history. Douglas Rights's *The American Indian in North Carolina* (1957) cites a source stating that, in the early 1700s, the Keyauwees united with the Saura Indians. The combined tribes moved toward the eastern section of the state and later united with the Cheraw or Catawba tribes. By the mid-1700s, when families of European descent first began arriving in the Piedmont area, most of the Native American population had moved elsewhere. Additionally, a smallpox epidemic in the late 1730s had greatly diminished the tribes. For her book, *Roanoke: Solving the Mystery of the Lost Colony* (2001), anthropologist Lee Miller intensively researched documents from Europe and America. She argues that the Roanoke colonists were not murdered (at least, not all of them) as some scholars contend, but eventually dispersed, with some colonists cohabiting with American Indian tribes, including those at the Keyauwee village. Many dispute Miller's thesis, and evidence is so scant that we may never know of the colonists' fate with any real certainty.

Among the region's early white settlers, who entered the Piedmont in significant numbers from the 1730s to the 1770s, were those who emigrated from Pennsylvania and Maryland—Germans, Scots-Irish, and English Quakers—piling their possessions in horse-drawn wagons or small carts. But many walked the arduous journey, taking from six weeks to three months, through Virginia's Shenandoah Valley. Most of these settlers shared the common goal of finding

Bishop August Gottlieb Spangenberg was responsible for establishing the Moravian settlement known as Wachovia in present-day Forsyth County. Photograph courtesy of the State Archives, North Carolina Office of Archives and History, Raleigh.

fertile and affordable land, a warmer climate, and freedom of religion. Another group of early settlers came from northeastern North Carolina, notably from Perquimans and Pasquotank counties, where desirable land was scarce and families were plagued by such coastal diseases as malaria.

In October 1752, Bishop August Gottlieb Spangenberg led a survey expedition of Moravians from Pennsylvania to a tavern and trading post known as Rich's on Caraway, built at the forks of Caraway Creek at a crossroads on the Great Trading Path; this is the earliest known established post of white settlers in the area. Spangenberg was searching for a permanent site for the Moravian community. In 1753, he purchased from John Carteret,

Lord Granville (1690-1763), one of the Lords Proprietors of Carolina, 98,985 acres in present-day Forsyth County and named the Moravian settlement Wachovia.

London merchant and land speculator Henry McCulloh advertised in the 1750s his "Tract No. 10," touting one hundred thousand acres available on "the Rich lands of the Uwharrie" and attracting eager settlers. Because an original stipulation accompanying the enormous land grants McCulloh had received required him to attract German-speaking Protestants to the colony, many of these settlers were of German origin; among them were Dunkers, or German Baptist Brethren, who opposed both formal education and organized politics and refused to declare any type of oath. This meant they could not participate in lawsuits or, in some cases, register deeds with the county court.

Between 1750 and 1761, a few landowners acquired thousands of acres of land through grants from Lord Granville, who had been unwilling to sell his share of Carolina back to the Crown in 1729. Most of the farms established on these lands were quite small. Early land purchases (1740-1770) included : Duncan McCullom, grant on Sandy Creek, 1746; Jeremiah Reynolds, 20 acres on Polecat Creek, 1753; Zebulan Gant, 632 acres on Deep River, 1753; Herman Husband, both sides of Deep River at Cedar Falls, 1755; Henry Ballinger, tract on Polecat Creek, 1755; Anthony Hoggett, 480 acres on Deep River, 1755; and Andreas Huber, tract on Uwharrie River, 1761. In 1777, the State of North Carolina confiscated Lord Granville's land because of his ties to the Crown, and from that point on settlers acquired land from the state.

In the early years of settlement, there were relatively few slaves in the Randolph area, especially when compared with many other Piedmont and eastern counties, where numerous large plantations existed. The vast majority of farms in the county were historically single-family farms; they did not require extra field hands, nor did families have the resources to support slaves. These farms produced subsistence levels of crops like wheat and corn.

With a steady climb in the number of inhabitants, Randolph stood poised for an awakening economy and other socioeconomic changes during the latter decades of the 1700s. Randolph witnessed several transforming developments, including the emergence of the first water-powered mills, the arrival of trained potters from England

and Germany, and a religious revival movement (one sweeping other regions of the country as well) known as the Great Awakening. This revival movement, which originated in New England in the 1730s, spread to the South during the next decade. At the expense of the old Puritan churches, the Baptist and Methodist (and to a lesser extent, Presbyterian) churches began a steady rise to eventual prominence. Moreover, by the 1770s, citizens' outrage concerning unscrupulous tax collectors had reached a pinnacle. Soon thereafter came the Revolutionary War.

In the two decades prior to and following the American Revolution, the first mills appeared in the Randolph area. In 1756, Samuel Walker erected the first gristmill on Sandy Creek; Andreas Huber built a mill at the forks of the Uwharrie in 1787; and John Barton constructed a mill on Stinking Quarter Creek in 1781. William Bell built a mill on Deep River about 1782, followed by Elisha Mendenhall building Coltrane's Mill on the same river about 1787. These mills constituted the first harnessing of waterpower in the area. By the late 1700s there were forty gristmills on the rivers and streams of the county.

In addition to installing the heavy round rock wheels for grinding corn and wheat, millers soon devised rigs for converting logs into lumber by utilizing this same waterpower. Later, as technology improved, waterpower was used to card wool (carding involves combing and disentangling fibers) and to crush flaxseed for making linseed oil. A few gristmills later used waterpower to turn lathes for the production of furniture parts.

Although the county's rivers and streams were not deep enough for vessels other than flat-bottomed skiffs or small boats, many residents—especially individuals who made their livelihoods as fishermen and those who fished to provide sustenance for their families—were not at all happy over the mills' damming of waterways. Interrupting the flow of water on the Uwharrie and Deep Rivers, fishermen claimed, adversely affected the supply of shad, eels, sturgeon, and other fish. Dams also prevented shad from swimming upstream from saltwater to spawn in freshwater. Therefore, on December 15, 1773, fishermen of these streams petitioned the colonial assembly, "praying a law may pass to facilitate the passage of Fish in Deep river." Specifically, they wanted a law requiring the mill owners to "affix proper flood gates in their dams from the mouth of said River to Field & Dicks Mill above the trading path and then to keep open at proper times from the tenth of February to the tenth of April that the said inhabitants may in some manner be Restored to their former priveledge of catching fish." The assembly declined to pass a law regulating dams, convinced that the products from the mills were more essential.

In the mid-1700s, new industries and trades stood ready to launch in Randolph. As early as 1740, trained potters, attracted by the extensive clay deposits, arrived in several sections of the future Randolph County—notably the Seagrove area, a generic appellation that encompasses parts of present-day Moore, Montgomery, and Lee counties. Many of the potters, including the Cole family, relocated from Virginia. The Coles had previously emigrated from England to Jamestown, where the Virginia Company of London had established various trades and crafts. George and William Cole moved to the Randolph area, attracted by the red and gray clays.

Other potters migrated to the region, many via the Great Wagon Road (which terminated in Georgia) from Philadelphia. Among them was the Fox family, who arrived in 1753 and settled a short distance south of today's Randolph-Moore county line. Other Fox sons followed. The family's potters employed various techniques and clays. Among their raw materials was iron-rich clay from a nearby bog, which gave their pottery pieces a darker hue. In contrast, clays from the Holly Spring area produced pottery of a lighter color. Potter Peter Craven settled near Coleridge on Blue Branch of Back Creek and established a shop. However, according to the 1820 census, he had moved to Chatham County, Indiana, where his four sons also were potters. Other early potters who settled around Seagrove included the Chriscoe, Owens, and Luck families.

Excavations in other sections of Randolph County prove the existence of other active potters during this period, notably a Moravian potter on Shepherd Mountain in Tabernacle Township and a Quaker potter originally from Old Salem in Forsyth County. The North Carolina Historical Exploration group joined local amateur archaeologists and potters for 1973 to 1975 excavations at Shepherd Mountain Retreat Center. Archaeologists found sherds and a stove tile that was later reproduced and designated a symbol for Randolph County's bicentennial celebration. The creator of these items has been identified as a Moravian potter named Jacob Meyer, who lived among the German settlers of Shepherd Mountain, circa 1797.

Excavations at New Salem, north of the town of Randleman, have uncovered not only pottery sherds dating to the colonial period, but also the second-oldest kiln discovered in the state—unique also in that it is linked to a Quaker potter. Pottery sherds found on the property of Hal Pugh include lead-glazed earthenware mugs, plates, and pitchers with geometric and floral designs similar to those of the early potters at Old Salem. These remnants date from 1780 to 1830. Pottery was not a full-time profession for most of these artisans; to support their families, many also engaged in farming and milling. Potters of this period created utilitarian wares such as jugs, crocks, churns, bowls, and dishes. If their inventories were greater than local demand, some would load wagons and travel to other areas to market their creations.

In addition to potters, religious groups settled the Randolph area in the mid-eighteenth century. In 1755, the Reverend Shubal Stearns arrived with a band of sixteen family members and neighbors, settling on a tract four miles northwest of the future town of Liberty, in Randolph's northeastern section. These Baptists migrated to this southern frontier following a disagreement with the established New England church about musical instruments and foreign missions. At their new settlement, the group established Sandy Creek Baptist Church, later recognized as the mother church of the Southern Baptist denomination. The church rapidly grew to six hundred members, and this congregation of Separate (Primitive) Baptists later established forty-two churches over a 250-mile radius.

North Carolinians organized the state Methodist Society in 1772, and soon thereafter circuit riders—among them Bishop Francis Asbury—brought their messages to the Randolph area. Bishop Asbury crossed Deep River in a skiff on July 25, 1780, and rode horseback to a settlement of about sixty people, where he proclaimed that he was at a loss whether to preach to "saints or sinners." (Bishop Asbury had not been in the vicinity long enough to develop a feeling for his audience.) Over the next three decades, the bishop preached in the area on several occasions, including in January 1790 at William McMaster's chapel. He wrote in his diary, "[W]e were speaking about four hours."

Sandy Creek Baptist Church, near the present-day town of Liberty, was established by followers of the Reverend Shubal Stearns of Boston, who led a group of sixteen families to the area in 1755. Sandy Creek is recognized as the mother church of the Southern Baptist denomination. Photograph courtesy of the State Archives.

Old Union Methodist, the oldest established Methodist church in the county, dates to 1802. It is widely recognized as the mother church of Methodism in Randolph County because other congregations branched from it. John McGee Jr., son of British army colonel John McGee and his wife Martha (see page 19), served as the first local Methodist preacher. Along with his brother William, a Presbyterian minister, McGee conducted the area's first camp meeting from late 1801 through January 1802 at Bell's Meeting, a log building constructed in 1786 for non-denominational worship.

Quakers—members of the Society of Friends—began moving into the North Carolina Piedmont in the 1740s, locating in present-day Randolph, Chatham, Guilford, Alamance, and Surry counties. Quakers were living on Deep River as early as 1758, and Providence Meeting was organized around 1762, with the first meetinghouse built around 1769. In that same year, Holly Spring Meeting was listed as a daughter to Orange County's Cane Creek Meeting. (Cane Creek Meeting is located in present-day Alamance County.)

This photo of the second meetinghouse of Back Creek Friends Meeting was taken some-time around the 1920s. Photograph courtesy of the Friends Historical Collection, Guilford College, Greensboro, N.C.

Other meetings followed: Uwharrie (prior to 1780), Back Creek (1785), and Marlborough (1797).

Among the early period's German population, settlers established Richland Lutheran Church in 1789, but the church soon became dormant because of the large number of German Lutherans who moved to western states. However, Richland members organized Melanchton Lutheran Church in 1827.

As North Carolina's population increased, citizens and officials noted a growing need for local government. In 1771, the colonial legislature established additional counties. (From 1754 to 1776, counties were also designated as parishes of the Anglican Church.) Guilford became a county in 1771, formed from portions of Orange (est. 1752) and Rowan (est. 1753) counties, with the High Sheriff (appointed by the royal governor) serving as chief executive officer of the court. The legislature established Randolph County, formed from the southern half of Guilford County, in 1779. In these and other newly established Piedmont counties, the highly centralized provincial government appointed the majority of local officials,

11

contributing to local citizens' belief that they lacked a voice in their government.

The colonial legislature imposed poll and property taxes and levied additional special taxes, a small number of which were designated for local government. Among the most unpopular of these taxes was one imposed in 1766 for constructing and furnishing Tryon Palace, the lavish and costly royal governor's estate in New Bern. Residents of the western part of the province expressed great indignation over these measures, organizing to protest what they deemed unfair taxation of the comparatively poor backcountry residents and the corruption and extortion tactics of many of the government-appointed local officials, such as sheriffs, who collected taxes for their fees. Some of the collectors, among them Edmund Fanning in Orange and John Frohock in Rowan, charged exorbitant collection fees for their services and became wealthy as a result.

Grievances over excessive taxes, illegal fees, corruption, and dishonest sheriffs served as the impetus for the Regulator movement, formally organized in 1765. The movement, as it coalesced and its adherents took action, became known as the War of the Regulation. Supported almost exclusively by "backwoods" citizens of the western part of the province, it derived its name from citizens' (most of them farmers) desires to "regulate" their own affairs, and to compel tax collectors to regulate taxes and collection fees in amounts specified by the legislature.

Herman Husband, a prominent citizen owning more than a thousand acres on Sandy Creek, became a spokesman for, and one of several unofficial leaders of, the Regulators from 1766 until 1771. A Quaker, Husband opposed the bearing of arms, disapproved of violence of any sort, and demonstrated his commitment to bringing about a peaceful solution by repeatedly petitioning provincial governor William Tryon for an audience. Finally, after some five hundred citizens of Orange County signed a petition, Tryon responded by demanding that the citizens pay their taxes as levied and cease their rebellion. However, Tryon promised to confer with Regulators in September 1768 in Hillsborough, where Edmund Fanning faced trial for extorting excessive fees. Herman Husband and William Butler—another leader in the Regulator movement—were also on trial, they for inciting the populace to rebellion. The court fined Fanning one penny plus costs, acquitted Husband, and

Edmund Fanning, Loyalist, colonial official, and British army general, was born in Long Island, N.Y. He earned degrees from Yale College and Harvard College. He eventually settled in Hillsborough, N.C., where he held various political posts. Over the years, he acquired large amounts of property across the state. Settlers were suspicious of his friendship with Gov. William Tryon and loathed Fanning in general. In fact, his house was targeted during a riot in September 1770, and Regulators assaulted him when they raided a session of superior court. Image courtesy of the State Archives.

convicted and sentenced Butler to fines and imprisonment. Never-theless, the Regulators were upset because Tryon had not addressed their complaints.

The Regulators became increasingly discouraged over the failure of negotiations to resolve their grievances. Reacting to more frequent incidents of violence and open defiance of the laws requiring payment of fees, the governor's council ordered Tryon to bring forth the provincial militia to move against the Regulators. In May 1771, Tryon dispatched some eleven hundred troops of the eastern militia to Great Alamance Creek, located west of Hillsborough in present-day Alamance County. The Regulators assembled there did not expect violence from Tryon and were unprepared for battle when his troops arrived on May 16. After the Regulators refused Tryon's terms of surrender, the militia, with cannons, riflemen, and cavalry, easily overwhelmed the disorganized Regulators, who lacked leadership and adequate munitions. Total casualties exceeded two hundred, with fewer than a dozen men killed on each side. A number of Regulators were buried at the site. Between twenty and thirty were taken prisoner. This skirmish, known as the Battle of Alamance, essentially quashed the rebellion.

On May 21, Tryon and his men burned the house and barn of James Hunter (the "general" of the Regulation), located on Sandy Creek. At Husband's estate they destroyed the manor house, crops, and all buildings. Husband, recognized as Randolph County's first Patriot, fled to Pennsylvania. Tryon offered a hundred pounds sterling and a thousand acres of land for the capture of Husband, who, over two decades later, was arrested and sentenced to death after becoming an active leader in the Whiskey Rebellion of 1794. Husband had found solidarity with the rebelling farmers of western Pennsylvania, whose violent opposition to the federal excise tax on liquor and stills resembled North Carolina's Regulator movement. President George Washington would later pardon Husband following the intercession of three North Carolinians—Presbyterian minister and teacher David Caldwell, U.S. senator and former governor Alexander Martin, and legislator Timothy Bloodworth. (Ironically, Martin had been assaulted by a Regulator mob when working as a lawyer in a Hillsborough court in 1770. He later negotiated with the rebels and agreed to refund excess fees. While serving in the state legislature, Martin introduced a bill to pardon Regulators.) Following his release from prison, Husband died peacefully in 1795 while resting in a tavern before resuming his journey home to Pennsylvania.

A number of Regulators faced trial in Hillsborough, and six were executed immediately, including James Pugh from Randolph. By mid-1771, more than three thousand Regulators had taken the oath of allegiance to the Crown, but many others left the province—an estimated fifteen hundred families that supported the Regulator movement moved to South Carolina and eastern Tennessee shortly after the Battle of Alamance. The Regulators achieved widespread publicity throughout the country, and many of the movement's aims were later incorporated into the state constitution. Moreover, when the Continental Congress formally endorsed the Declaration of Independence on July 4, 1776, it cited principles and grievances similar to those the Regulators had fought for at the Battle of Alamance.

Following the Battle of Alamance, six Regulators were hanged. This plaque, located at Alamance Battleground State Historic Site, depicts the execution of James Pugh. Courtesy of Alamance Battleground.

In examining statewide political sentiments during this era, one can identify three distinct groups based on their loyalties, beliefs, and convictions. First there were the Whigs, probably consisting of about half the population of Randolph, who were willing to fight England for redress of grievances and possibly even for independence. Most of the small farmers and artisans belonged to this group, but a number of large landowners also were among their numbers. The Loyalists (or Tories, as they were commonly called) supported peaceful opposition to British policies, but opposed war at all costs. This group included many of the wealthy merchants, most of the old officials who had served as officers of the royal government, and some former Regulators, who harbored harsh feelings from their defeat at Alamance but remembered the oaths of allegiance they had taken to get back in the good graces of the royal government. The third and smaller group were neutrals and consisted primarily of Quakers, Moravians, and Dunkers (all of whom were against bearing arms), and a large percentage of the other German settlers.

They were "taxed fourfold" by the local authorities as an exemption penalty for refusing to participate in the fighting—a less harsh penalty than having their lands subjected to confiscation.

Andrew Hoover (anglicized from Andreas Huber) was among the individual Quakers who made a payment of five hundred dollars to the Revolutionary cause rather than fight. He had come to this country from Ellerstadt in the Palatinate (in present-day southwestern Germany) in 1723 and soon thereafter moved to the Randolph area. He was born to Huguenot parents but became a Quaker in Philadelphia where he married Margaret Pfautz. Andrew Hoover was a great-great-grandfather of Herbert Hoover, the thirty-first president of the United States. The Hoovers acquired approximately two hundred acres on the east side of the Uwharrie River and established a gristmill, which they used to saw logs when there was no grain to grind. The Hoovers and six other families decided to leave the area following two devastating floods; their opposition to slavery and the availability of large tracts of good, inexpensive farmland in the western provinces probably factored into that decision. The family eventually settled in Ohio.

Following the Revolutionary War's initial 1775 battles in the Northeast, the war spread to the South, with skirmishes in Virginia. Fighting reached eastern North Carolina in February 1776 when a force of North Carolina Patriots defeated Scottish Loyalists at Moore's Creek Bridge, near Wilmington. In the Randolph area, the war years (1775-1782) constituted an era of bitter internal strife, although there were no major battles in the immediate vicinity. There are no complete records showing how many men Randolph provided for the Continental army, or even how many served in the militia. The list of those receiving pensions for service in either category numbered more than 100 of the 6,086 statewide. Notable among these Continental army soldiers was Capt. William Clark, who lived at Naomi on the south side of Deep River and was widely regarded as a Patriot. Clark, the leader of the Whig Party in the area, achieved recognition for having captured and executed John Elrod and Samuel Still, two notorious Tories who lived at the forks of the Yadkin River, some fifty miles to the west. Three of Clark's brothers also served as captains in the Continental army.

The Whigs and neutrals had to maintain constant vigils to protect their lives and property from another notorious Tory, Col. David Fanning, who was appointed by the British in 1781 to command the Loyal Militia of Randolph and Chatham counties (some six hundred men). Fanning, born in Virginia, grew up in present-day Johnston County, North Carolina. He was extremely loyal to the Crown, was confident of eventual British victory, and believed he stood well positioned to become the military governor of North Carolina. His personal journals reflect his brilliance and boastfulness. One of Fanning's victims, Andrew Balfour, came to the area in 1778 and purchased about four thousand acres on Betty McGee Creek (near the Asheboro Municipal Airport). He served as a member of the legislature, a justice of the peace, and a colonel in the Randolph militia. On March 10, 1782, Fanning and his Tories murdered Balfour at his farm. After plundering Balfour's plantation, Fanning rode to William Millikan's residence on Deep River and burned the house, then proceeded to Capt. John Burns's and destroyed his house. President Washington would later appoint Balfour's widow, Elizabeth Dayton Balfour, postmistress in Salisbury, North Carolina, the first female in the country to hold that office.

There were many such violent incidents in North Carolina and Virginia, compounding the terror wreaked by David Fanning. Just weeks after Balfour's murder, on May 2, 1782, Fanning confronted Andrew Hunter, a Patriot who had been taken prisoner by the British but had broken parole. Fanning threatened to hang Hunter on the spot but instead stationed a sentinel to guard him while Fanning examined Hunter's papers. Recognizing the dire situation, Hunter seized the moment, jumping on Bay Doe (Fanning's favorite horse, which was grazing nearby) and galloping away as his captors fired four shots. A fifth shot struck Hunter in the fleshy part of his shoulder, disabling his arm. While Hunter was in Salisbury having the bullet removed, Fanning plundered Hunter's home on Little River and absconded with the pregnant Mrs. Hunter, all eight of the family's horses, and three young male slaves, holding them for ransom in return for Bay Doe, Fanning's personal papers, and his brace of pistols, which were in the saddlebag. A legendary, and perhaps apocryphal, story says that Hunter escaped capture by jumping Bay Doe from Faith Rock at Franklinville into Deep River, some sixty feet below. The horse and rider swam to safety. This story is often told even today in the area.

After America and Great Britain signed a peace treaty in 1783, Fanning traveled to Charleston, booked passage on a ship, and settled in Nova Scotia, where he died in 1825. Before leaving, Fanning described in his *Narrative* some of the hardships of the Tory families whose men served in his British militia, noting that their "properties real and personal [were] taken to support their enemies—the fatherless and widows stripped, and every means of support taken from them." Fanning stated that some of the Tories left for the West Indies and other foreign locations. He also expressed sorrow over the plight of two of his Tory officers—Maj. John Rains and Capt. George Rains—whom he described as the "diservingest officers that ever acted in America." Fanning wrote of the burning of John Rains's two mills, three dwellings, and barn by citizens directing their ire at Loyalists. Other Tory officers, hoping to be pardoned under 1783's Act of Pardon and Oblivion, were hanged in Hillsborough when they returned to America. The act did not pardon Tories who had taken part in heinous crimes.

Though Randolph County saw no major military engagements during the Revolutionary War, Gen. Johann de Kalb of the Continental army reached Deep River and bivouacked for about two weeks at Cox's Mill. He departed on July 25, 1780, when Gen. Horatio Gates, recently commissioned as leader of the Southern Army, replaced de Kalb in command. Gates ordered a salute of eight artillery pieces in de Kalb's honor—the only artillery fired in this Quaker community during the war. In actuality, there were two Cox's Mills: one at Buffalo Ford operated by Thomas Cox and, less than a mile away, another at Millstone Creek run by Harmon Cox, Thomas's brother. It is likely that de Kalb remained in the area for such a lengthy period because the two mills provided much-needed supplies for the fourteen hundred soldiers camped along the river. Even with this bonanza, the Continental army suffered from a lack of food and supplies. After reinforcement troops completed their arduous march to North Carolina, Gates moved his men to Camden, South Carolina, where, in August, they were routed by British general Lord Charles Cornwallis's troops.

Another section of the Continentals, under Gen. Isaac Huger, left their station at Cheraw, South Carolina, and passed through Randolph on their way to join Gen. Nathanael Greene in March 1781 at the Battle of Guilford Courthouse, staged north of present-day Greensboro, North Carolina. Greene's and Cornwallis's armies met on March 15. Intense fighting ensued, and the Continentals twice turned back the British, who suffered heavy losses—a quarter of Cornwallis's men were killed or seriously wounded. Cornwallis brought back fresh troops and prepared for another assault, but Greene withdrew, satisfied with the damage he had inflicted.

Lord Charles Cornwallis and his British troops camped for two days at William and Martha McGee Bell's plantation following the Battle of Guilford Courthouse. Image courtesy of the State Archives.

Following the Battle of Guilford Courthouse, and before his retreat to Wilmington, General Cornwallis camped for two days at the Sandy Creek plantation of William Bell, Randolph County's first sheriff. Bell served as a scout for General Greene and as the appointed commissary to furnish supplies for the North Carolina militia. His second wife, Martha McGee Bell, kept the plantation and gristmill operating in the absence of her husband, who had to keep out of sight because he was wanted by the Tories. Martha Bell's first husband was a colonel in the British army, but after his death in 1773 she became a supporter of American independence. On many occasions, she scouted for the Randolph militia and the Continental army, and administered to the needs of the wounded. Neighbors described her as a woman "who feared her maker, but nothing on earth."

Walker's Mill, owned by Samuel Walker, on Muddy Creek in New Market Township was originally the site of Capt. William Bell's mill. General Cornwallis camped here for several days before continuing his retreat to Wilmington after the Battle of Guilford Courthouse. Lord Cornwallis encountered yet another formidable opponent in the feisty Mrs. Bell, whose spirited defiance, it is said, may have swayed the British from torching her home and gristmill. Photograph courtesy of the Randolph County Public Library.

When Cornwallis arrived at the Bells' plantation, Martha convinced him that she did not know the whereabouts of her husband, who was hiding nearby. She then inquired as to the general's intentions after he informed her that he planned to use her entire plantation as his headquarters and her mill to grind her corn for his men. According to legend, after Cornwallis assured her that he did not intend to torch her property, Martha informed him that if he had such intentions, she was fully prepared and capable of burning the property herself to deny him the use of it. Before leaving, the British plundered the farm, seizing grain, cattle, and whatever goods they could carry but spared the house and gristmill.

Other female Patriots of the Randolph area achieved recognition for their compassion and courageous acts during the American

Martha McGee Bell is memorialized by this marker in the Bell–Welborn Cemetery on Deep River in Randolph County. The Guilford Battle Chapter National Society of the Daughters of the American Revolution placed it on September 11, 1997. Photograph by the author.

Revolution. Hannah Blair, a Quaker who lived south of New Market, often delivered food and messages to hidden troops. Twice she saved men by hiding them. Betty McGee and her family lived on Col. Andrew Balfour's plantation, and as a trained nurse, she followed the Continental army into several battles, including the Battle of Guilford Courthouse, where she rode horseback to the scene and nursed the wounded in the old New Garden meetinghouse.

For Cornwallis, the Battle of Guilford Courthouse was a Pyrrhic victory. The British troops, greatly weakened, marched to the North Carolina coast at Wilmington. Cornwallis later began a slow march through eastern North Carolina, progressing toward Yorktown, Virginia. Along the route, Cornwallis's troops and loyal followers wreaked havoc on the countryside, burning houses and seizing residents' property.

On October 19, 1781, at Yorktown, the British army suffered defeat at the hands of General Washington's troops and their French allies. Eight thousand British troops lay down their arms, effectively dashing any British hopes for overall victory. In 1782, the troops began their withdrawal from the colonies, and in 1783 the two countries signed a peace treaty. Upon gaining independence from Britain, Randolph County residents were eager to make amends with neighbors and move forward in unity, leaving behind the ill will and strife of the war years. The coming decades would pose new challenges, further testing their fortitude.

CHAPTER TWO

Independence and
a New County Established

*I*n 1778, during the midst of the Revolutionary War, citizens of the southern half of Guilford County petitioned the North Carolina General Assembly to create a new county, arguing that the "great distance to Guilford Court House rendered it grievous and troublesome to the inhabitants thereof to attend the courts, assemblies, elections and other public meetings." The assembly of 1779 passed an act forming a new county, naming it "Randolph" in honor of Peyton Randolph of Virginia, who twice served as president of the Continental Congress. The act appointed Thomas Owen, Col. John Collier, John Adineal, Jacob Sheppard, James Martin, and William Dent to survey the proposed Guilford-Randolph county line. It also appointed Absalom Tatom, William Cole, John Hinds, John Collier, and William Bell as commissioners for determining the most convenient place for erecting the courthouse, prison, and stocks.

As provided by the act, the first court of pleas and quarter sessions convened at the home of Abraham Reece, on present-day U.S. 311 about halfway between Brown's Crossroads and Randleman. The court's justices were nominated by their peers and appointed by the governor, rather than elected by the people. It was authorized to hear the following: civil actions based on contracts, where the sum did not exceed forty shillings; petty larcenies; assaults and batteries; and other minor offenses and misdemeanors. The court also appointed the overseers of roads, took probate of deeds, granted letters of administration and letters testamentary, licensed tavern keepers, and fixed tavern rates. The court largely performed the same administrative functions as today's county board of commissioners. Absalom Tatom was unanimously elected county clerk, and William Bell sheriff. William Millikan was elected "registerer" for the county.

John Collier took his oath as lieutenant colonel of the Randolph regiment of militia. The following were appointed justices for holding court: John Arnold, William Bell, William Cole, John Collier, George Cortner, Enoch Davis, John Hinds, Joseph Hinds, James Hunter, John Lowe, William Merrell, William Millikan, Richardson Owen, Windsor Peirce, William Plunket, and Jacob Sheppard.

Another figure in Randolph's early history, Jeduthan Harper, moved to the area during the latter part of the Revolutionary War. He purchased from the commissioners of confiscated property nearly a thousand acres in Trinity Township. The parcel, previously owned by Henry Eustace McCulloh, was known as the Richlands. The state government had confiscated McCulloh's land, in addition to sixty-seven estates belonging to other large landowners in North Carolina who were singled out in an act of 1779 as being loyal to the Crown.

Also notable in 1779, the first county tax list showed 879 taxables in Randolph. The list indicated that, with an average of five persons per family, the population at the formation of the county stood at approximately forty-five hundred. Three initial court sessions convened at the home of Abraham Reece. At this time a small log house for hosting the court was under construction on land owned by Stephen Rigdon, at a crossroads where the old trading path (Salisbury-Hillsborough Road) intersected the road running from Cross Creek to Salem, a location where the weekly stage brought mail and passengers. A two-story courthouse later replaced the log house. Tom Dougan donated a hundred acres to the county, and the new county seat located thereon was to be known as Johnstonville as a tribute to Samuel Johnston, the governor of the state at the time. Johnstonville thrived for about fourteen years, with some seventy-five lots purchased and homes built, along with stores, hotels, barrooms, and the shops of cobblers, blacksmiths, furniture makers, and hatters.

Records of the earliest court sessions show that the sheriff and his deputies were ordered to attend court with their swords on, and three constables were required to arm themselves with six-foot-long sticks to maintain order. During one early session, the court fined Col. William Moore fifty pounds for contempt for "riding his horse into the court house during the sitting of court." The court ordered Moore jailed until he paid the fine.

Reports described Johnstonville as a lively place for commerce as well as social events, with frequent horse races, sporting events, and biannual county fairs. It was into this environment that Andrew Jackson (the future seventh president of the United States) arrived on December 11, 1787. The tall, gangly Jackson presented his license as a practicing attorney, qualifying before justices John Arnold, Zebedee Wood, John Lane, and Aaron Hill. The documents signed by Jackson at this court session were his first cases on record as an attorney. He had received his license after reading law under attorneys at Salisbury and upon examination on September 26, 1787, by judges Samuel Ashe and John F. Williams, who found Jackson "a person of unblemished moral character, and . . . competent . . . [with] knowledge of the law."

Court records, and Jackson's reputation, provide clues about his possible activities and whereabouts shortly after arriving in Johnstonville. An "A. Jackson" signed court documents in March 1788, verifying that he represented a client (the records indicated no specific date). Given this signature and the fact that Andrew Jackson was born March 15, 1767, it is highly likely that he was in Johnstonville on his twenty-first birthday and eager to celebrate—residents of nearby Salisbury recognized him as "the most roaring, rollicking, game-cocking, horse-racing, card-playing, mischievous fellow, that ever lived in Salisbury [and] the head of the rowdies hereabouts." Jackson departed Randolph County soon after

Andrew Jackson, while very young, served as a courier for Gen. William R. Davie during the Revolutionary War. He and a brother were briefly imprisoned by the British. He eventually settled in Tennessee where he began his political career, and was elected president in 1828 and reelected in 1832. Photograph courtesy of the State Archives.

the March term of court, eventually establishing his home in Tennessee.

Johnstonville gradually declined, and no trace remains of this once-thriving village. Other sections of the county began to gain population, and citizens complained that the courthouse was too far away (the same complaint that had caused Guilford County to be divided). Residents sought to establish the new county seat at the geographical center of the county. Surveys concluded that this central point lay within a two-hundred-acre tract acquired in 1786 by Jesse Henley. The tract's only inhabitant was an old man named Abram who lived in a small cabin. In 1793 Henley conveyed, for ten shillings, two acres of land on Abram's Creek, and on June 12, 1796, the first court convened in a small building on newly cleared land. The first courthouse built was a large two-story frame building.

On Christmas Day 1796, the General Assembly ratified legislation establishing "a town on the lands of Jesse Henley in the County of Randolph at the courthouse of said county," noting also that Henley had consented to have fifty acres "laid off" for a town with one-acre lots. Commissioners named to execute the task were Jesse Henley Jr., Phineas Nixon, Samuel Trogdon, Henry Ransower, and Joseph Brown. The assembly appointed John Harvey treasurer for public buildings. The new county seat, Asheboro, was named for New Hanover County's Samuel Ashe, who was a distinguished soldier of the American Revolution, a superior court justice, and governor of North Carolina from 1795 to 1798. The town's name has been spelled several different ways over the years. First it was "Asheborough," then "Ashboro," and the present "Asheboro" was adopted after U.S. representative William Cicero Hammer of Asheboro persuaded the postal service to standardize the name. The name "Asheboro" became official on January 10, 1923. From its establishment in 1796 until the beginning of the nineteenth century, Asheboro's chief reason for existence was the county court. Because the town had no waterpower, it had no industry. Rather, the working population consisted primarily of county officials, lawyers, a few merchants and craftsmen, and individuals whose businesses— such as barrooms, livery stables, hotels, and shoe shops—catered to the courts.

Randolph County's initial entry into the regional and national marketplace occurred a bit earlier, around 1785. Because the many streams in Randolph County were suitable for only shallow-draft boats, anyone engaged in major intra- or interstate commerce was compelled to transport goods overland to a major river: either to Fayetteville for transport down the Cape Fear River to Wilmington, or to Cheraw, South Carolina, for shipment down the Great Pee Dee River to Charleston. (The construction of the North Carolina Railroad in the 1850s, which shifted the primary trade routes to Greensboro and High Point, would bring forth the demise of this system.) Shipments of flour, tobacco, lard, and whiskey arrived in the Fayetteville market in exchange for salt, coffee, sugar, spices, iron, and other items. Later, tanneries and potteries utilized this same method to market their goods. Cotton, too, soon established itself as a major commodity. By 1802 there were five cotton gins in Randolph, and the cotton, after being processed and spun, was ready to be woven into cloth. The 1810 tax listing shows 1,333 handlooms, 400 spindles, and 14 spinning frames producing 86,000 yards of a rather coarse handwoven cotton cloth worth a total of approximately $34,000, or about 40¢ a yard.

The first of five early cotton mills appeared when "Colonel" Benjamin Elliott, a highly respected citizen, attorney, and operator of a general merchandise store in Asheboro, decided to cut out the middleman by manufacturing his own yarns. In the mid-1820s Elliott purchased a tract on Deep River where the river dropped some fifty feet within a half mile. He hired workers to build a dam and sawmill, powered by an undershot flutter wheel, to produce flour and lumber.

On February 1, 1829, the General Assembly incorporated the Manufacturing Company of the County of Randolph, listing as principals Ben Elliott, clerk of the county court Hugh McCain, New Salem merchant Jesse Walker, and Jonathan Worth (future governor). The owners installed a single spindle at their mill, but because of a dearth of local citizens willing to invest in the new venture, the project briefly fell into dormancy. Henry Branson Elliott, a recent graduate of the University of North Carolina and Princeton Law School, returned home and formed a partnership with his father Ben and another father-son team, Dr. Philip Horney and Alexander S. Horney. The new management made the project at the mill, called Cedar Falls, a resounding success. Suppliers shipped equipment to the site via rail to Greensboro, with wagons

Sapona Cotton Mill (background) began as Cedar Falls Manufacturing Company, which was organized in 1836 and built in 1837 by Benjamin and Henry Elliott, and Dr. Philip and Alexander S. Horney. The original wooden building was replaced in 1846 by a three-story brick building. The Cedar Falls Covered Bridge (foreground) spanned the Deep River. This photograph was taken in 1930. Photograph courtesy of the Randolph County Public Library.

transporting it from there to the mill. By June 1837 there were five hundred spindles producing "superior quality cotton yarn."

Cedar Falls owners built houses for the employees in a newly developed village nearby. This mill village contained a company store well stocked with food, clothing, and general merchandise. Employees worked twelve-hour shifts beginning at 6:00 A.M. and 6:00 P.M. The mills remained idle at times when waterpower was lacking, but the advent of steam turbines in 1844 rectified this problem. The mill employed many children, especially in departments that did not require skilled laborers. Older girls threaded looms, a task requiring great dexterity. Wages ranged from three dollars per week for children to fifteen dollars for overseers. After a day of monotonous work, the people found companionship with village neighbors. Employees devoted free time on Saturday afternoons and on Sundays to church services, recreation, and socializing. Mill managers, and most employees, frowned upon dancing, card playing, and alcoholic beverages. There existed a camaraderie among the workers and owners, who knew all employees by name.

In his book *From the Cotton Field to the Cotton Mill* (1906), Holland Thompson notes that the five cotton mills built in Randolph

These houses sit on a ridge above the Sapona Cotton Mill. Such housing was typical for mill employees. Photograph courtesy of the Randolph County Public Library.

before 1850 were somewhat distinct: they were built by stock companies in a region containing a strong Quaker presence and a small number of slaves. Furthermore, neighborhood residents, as well as residents along Deep River and in the Asheboro area, owned shares.

The Cedar Falls factory (1836), later called Sapona Cotton Mill, acted as a catalyst for further industrialization in the county. Within the next year, ten men organized a large mill in a brick building, downriver at Franklinsville (1838), producing yarn and later adding looms. A third mill came in 1846 and was also built at Franklinsville. This mill manufactured seamless bags on two hundred looms. In 1848 citizens at Dicks (now Randleman) on Deep River created Union Manufacturing Company for operating a cotton mill. Two years later a factory made of brick was completed on Deep River at Allen's Fall, a town later called Columbia and known today as Ramseur. This mill employed about twenty people utilizing looms to weave cloth thirty-six inches wide.

> According to Holland Thompson, there was little or no prejudice against mill labor in this region, where men had traditionally been tillers of the soil and women were relegated to the duties of farmwives. Farmers' daughters gladly came to work in the mills; some young women continued to live at home and walked to the mills daily, while others boarded in the village with relatives or friends. Thompson further notes that "mill managers were men of high character, who felt themselves to stand in a parental relation to the operatives and required the observance of decorous conduct. Many girls worked to buy trousseaus, others to help their families. They lost no caste by working in the mills."

In order for industrialization and commerce to expand in Randolph County, individuals and business operations would require access to improved and expanded means of transportation. In the mid-1800s the state undertook measures to improve transportation, and Randolph eventually benefited. The General Assembly in the 1830s began chartering private railroad companies and authorized them to sell stock for funding. The state provided aid for these ventures. Railroad companies utilized both paid and slave labor for the construction of rail lines, which by 1860 in North Carolina totaled 891 miles.

The first railroads in the state—the Wilmington and Raleigh (161 miles long; later renamed the Wilmington and Weldon) and the Raleigh and Gaston (86 miles long)—were completed in 1840. At the time, the Wilmington and Raleigh was the longest railroad in the world. Neither extended into the Piedmont. (Raleigh was the westernmost point reached, served only by the Raleigh and Gaston.) In 1856 workers completed construction of the state-owned North Carolina Railroad; the state financed two-thirds, and stock purchases by private citizens financed the remaining one-third. This 223-mile-long route was the first railroad serving the Piedmont and connected Goldsboro and Charlotte, with stops in Raleigh, Hillsborough, Greensboro, Salisbury, and Concord. Former governor John Motley Morehead of Guilford County, the North Carolina Railroad's leading proponent, acted as its first president. Prior to the 1890 completion of the Cape Fear and Yadkin Valley Railway, which passed through Randolph County, the nearest railheads to Randolph by 1860 were: to the east, the Western Railroad terminus at Egypt (later known as Cumnock), on Deep River in present-day Lee County; and to the north and west, the North Carolina Railroad running through Guilford and Davidson counties to the station in Salisbury, in Rowan County. Completion of the Cape Fear and Yadkin Valley Railway added greatly to the development of the lumber industry in the southern regions of Randolph and also to the thriving textile mills along Deep River. Farmers also found the railroad an expedient and cost-effective means for shipping their products to market.

Although expanded rail service was a great advancement, it did not resolve all the county's transportation issues. The rocky, rugged terrain, dense tree cover, and undergrowth of the Piedmont region

NORTH CAROLINA RAILROAD.
TRAINS GOING EAST.

Date, May 15, '81	No 47 Daily	No 45 Daily	No 6 Daily ex Sunday
Leave Charlotte	3 50 a m	4 10 p m	
Salisbury	6 30	5 45	
High Point	7 30	7 06	
Ar. at Greensboro	8 20	7 37	
Leave Greensboro	8 10		0 00 p m
Arrive at Hillsbo'	10 23		1 22
Durham	11 02		1 17 a m
Raleigh	12 20 pm		3 00
Leave Raleigh	3 30	6 00 a m	
Arrive Goldsboro	6 00	10 00	

No 47—Connects at Salisbury with the W. N. C. R. R. for all points in Western North Carolina except Sundays. At Greensboro with the Richmond and Danville Road for all points North, East and West. At Goldsboro with the Wilmington and Weldon Road for Wilmington.

No 45—Connects at Greensboro with the R. & D. Railroad for all points North, East and West.

TRAINS GOING WEST.

Date, May 15, '81	No 4 Daily	No 42 Daily	No 5 daily ex Sunday
Leave Greensbo'	10 10am	6 34 am	
Arrive Raleigh	12 25pm	10 45	
Leave Raleigh	3 40pm		7 00 a m
Arrive Durham	4 52		9 19
Hillsboro	5 30		11 07
Greensbo	7 50		3 45
Leave Greensbo'	8 20	6 56 am	
Ar. High Point	8 55	7 30	
Salisbury	10 16	9 15	
Charlotte	12 27pm	11 17	

No 48—Connects at Greensboro with Salem Branch, at Air-Line Junction with A. & C. A. L. Railroad to all points South and Southwest, at Charlotte with the C. C. & A. Road for all points South and Southeast. At Salisbury with W. N. C. Road, daily except Sundays, for all points in Western North Carolina.

No 42—Connects at Air-Line Junction with A. C. A. L. Railroad for all points South and Southwest.

SALEM BRANCH.

Lv. Greensboro daily except Sunday		8 50 p. m.
Ar. Kernersville	" "	10 00
Arrive at Salem	" "	10 50
Leave Salem	" "	5 00 a. m.
Ar. Kernersville	" "	5 40
Ar. Greensboro'	" "	7 00

Connecting at Greensboro with trains on the R. & D. R. R. and N. C. R. R.

☞Through Tickets on sale at Greensboro, Raleigh, Goldsboro, Salisbury and Charlotte and at all principal points South, Southwest, West, North and East. For emigrant rates to points in Arkansas and Texas, address

J. R. MacMURDO,
Gen. Pass. Agent, Richmond, Va.

had historically proven troublesome for travelers, many of whom were farmers and merchants. These Piedmont businessmen and farmers, among others, sought other transportation options for these areas lacking rail service. Consequently, they were strong proponents of a controversial 1850s movement to build plank roads in the state. Popular in other states, the roads consisted of cleared roadways topped with wooden planks, providing travelers (primarily in wagons) a smooth surface free from mud, deep sand, and other obstacles. Opponents, however, pointed out that plank roads deteriorated rapidly and that maintenance was difficult and expensive. Eventually private companies, aided by the

This train schedule for the North Carolina Railroad was in effect on May 15, 1881. Note the directive at the bottom stating, "For emigrant rates to points in Arkansas and Texas, address J. R. MacMurdo, Gen. Pass. Agent, Richmond, Va.," reflecting the migration to these states at the time by many North Carolinians. Photograph courtesy of the State Archives.

state, constructed the plank roads, the majority of which appeared between 1849 and 1856. The plank road companies, chartered and partially funded by the state, were also financially supported by stock held by farmers and businessmen residing in areas served by the roads. Plank roads, at an average construction cost of fifteen hundred dollars per mile in North Carolina, cost about one-tenth as much as railroads and provided convenient all-weather transportation to railroads and waterways that reached markets outside the region. In the mid-1850s more than six hundred miles of railroads and approximately five hundred miles of plank roads existed statewide.

Although it had a life span of only fifteen years and totaled only 129 miles, the plank road passing through Randolph County aided the development of the area's business and industrial potential. Chartered in 1849, the Fayetteville and Western Plank Road, as it was officially named, was assigned other names depending on whether or not one favored it: "Appian Way of North Carolina," "the farmers' railroad," or "a monument of folly." Among the private contractors was New Salem's Jesse Walker, contracted to build a seven-mile stretch. Tollgates and houses for the keeper and his family lay approximately every eleven miles along the Fayetteville and Western, with fees beginning at a half cent per mile for a person

Wagons travel along a plank road in Randolph County. The exact location is unknown. Photograph courtesy of the Randolph County Public Library.

on horseback. The route extended from Fayetteville through High Point and Salem to Bethania in Forsyth County. Along the way, it entered Randolph County, passing near the county's first tollhouse, known as Page's (the residence of James Page and family), near the Moore-Randolph county line. Other tollhouses were located at Asheboro, New Market, and Archdale. The Fayetteville and Western was ten feet wide, slightly wider than most other plank roads in the state. In Randolph, builders used a mobile, steam-driven sawmill (the first in the county) to cut planks at the site, and crews laid stringers (heavy sills used to support the planks) in trenches parallel to the roadway. Workers secured the planks, usually made of pine, to the tops of the stringers and covered the surface with a layer of sand.

Randolph farmers extensively utilized the plank road to transport their produce southeast to Fayetteville. Piedmont farmers traveling there via the dry and dust-free road could sell their produce in the Coastal Plain town, reaping twice the profit margin versus home markets, even after paying tolls. Many traveled to market when weather rendered it difficult to work in the fields. Some spent the night on the road near their wagons, others at a roadside inn. In spite of the usage, the Fayetteville and Western failed to turn a profit for investors in Randolph County and elsewhere in the state. With its demise in the 1860s, farmers found it more convenient to travel north to markets in High Point along the remnants of the decaying plank road, or to Greensboro, along the mail route.

The expansion of railroads contributed to the roads' demise by making them less essential. Moreover, costly maintenance and the economic downturn accompanying the nationwide panic of 1857 also took their toll. Plank road companies and the fragile roads they built essentially disappeared, falling into disrepair and rotting away.

Generally speaking, the prevalence of small farms and an atmosphere of antagonism toward slavery accounted for the relative scarcity of the institution in Randolph County. Prior to 1840, slavery was limited in the county because a majority of the landowners held small farms, requiring considerably less labor than the large plantations nearer the coastal regions of the Carolinas. Few reliable sources of information exist concerning the numbers of slaves and free blacks and their treatment and living conditions prior to 1779, when Randolph became a separate political entity. The 1780 tax list listed Randolph's population at 3,801, with 227 slaves and 24 free "persons of color." The federal census of 1790 indicated a county population of 7,276, of whom 452

> The census of 1840 gives an indication of the county's early agriculture: corn was the leading field crop, with a production of 295,828 bushels, followed by 79,095 bushels of wheat; 47,671 bushels of oats; 91,533 pounds of cotton; 80,208 pounds of tobacco; and 17,636 pounds of wool.

were slaves. The tax listing of 1815 showed 1,543 entries. Of this number, 1,161 were listed as white (taxable males aged 16 to 50, consisting both of property owners and those owning no property) and 511 as black. Males over the age of 50 only made the list if they owned property.

Early court records indicate that indentured white orphans provided the much-needed labor that slaves provided in other locales. Homeless white boys were indentured to skilled craftsmen until age twenty-one and learned such trades as blacksmithing, boot making, carpentry, and saddle making.

Another significant factor limiting the number of slaves in the county was the influence of the large number of Quakers, who had adopted a dictum in the early 1770s urging Friends to limit their purchases of slaves and to prevent the separation of slave families. An 1818 incident reflects the sympathy of one local Quaker toward his own slaves. Rather than subjecting them to possible capture and enslavement upon his release of them, Abraham Simmons filed a deed in county court transferring his rights to a thirty-eight-year-old female slave and her seven children to three men acting as trustees for the North Carolina Yearly Meeting of Friends. This transaction recognized these eight former slaves as property of the church. It did not, however, guarantee unscrupulous people would honor the pronouncement, and unfortunately, there are no known records relating how Simmons's former slaves were treated from the time of their release until federal emancipation.

A similar incident appears in an excerpt from the autobiography of Randolph resident Alexander Spencer, describing an occurrence that happened around 1846. The passage reflects his sentiments about slavery:

Well, the next occurrence of note was the negro girl. I sold my farm of 160 acres for $200 to a man by the name of Hudson. He offered me a negro girl of 6 or 7 years old for the debt. I did not want to take her, but Noah Smitherman told me he would give $200 for her. I offered to take $180 for her rather than have my hands stained with a negro. Her name was Mary and she may be living yet for all I know. I went and got her and executed a deed for the land and received a bill of sale for the negro.

That night my wife cried nearly all night and I did not feel pleasant. Why I was always so sensitive about the negro was because I always thought it wrong to own and work them as slaves. My grandfather Spencer owned a good many slaves and I expected some of them would reach me sometime and I studied what I should do with them. I thought it was wrong to sell them or keep them as slaves. I need not to have seen any trouble. They got to my father, but the civil war came on and freed them and I thought it was right. Now you see why I had rather have $180 in money than $200 in a negro.

Even though in practice he did not totally disentangle himself from the buying and selling of slaves, Alexander Spencer, like a majority of Randolph County citizens, held some form of antislavery beliefs.

The Society of Friends (Quakers) was a powerful force in Randolph and a great influence in opposing slavery. When the state conducted a post-Civil War referendum to abolish slavery, for example, county residents voted 720 for and 28 against.

Prior to 1840, there were few schools in North Carolina where a student could achieve a classical education. The closest to Randolph County was Dr. David Caldwell's Log College in Greensboro. Itinerant teachers went from home to home when parents could afford to pay for tutoring. The Quakers and some other religious groups set up schools to accompany their churches.

In 1839 the General Assembly approved the state's first common school law. For a county to become eligible to enter the program, its voters were required to endorse the law's provisions, which called for the establishment of school districts. Seven counties declined, but Randolph was among the seventy-two that endorsed the measure, voting 847 for and 515 against. Randolph County was divided into twenty-one districts, each one nine miles north-to-south and four miles east-to-west. The county court appointed district superintendents, and that group chose Jonathan Worth county superintendent, a post he held for twenty years, from 1840 to 1860.

The General Assembly had passed a bill in 1825 creating the Literary Fund for the benefit of common schools. The program suffered years of setbacks and a lack of political support. An executive board was charged with investing the often meager funds and distributing the money to counties in proportion to their populations. Beginning in 1840, for every twenty dollars raised by each district the state Literary Fund provided forty dollars, giving each district an allowance of sixty dollars; in most counties the sum proved sufficient to operate the common schools for three months annually. The districts raised funds for school buildings, and the state provided forty dollars toward each teacher's salary. In Randolph, because of the need for children to work as farm laborers, the schools usually operated during the dormant season. School districts possessed the latitude to choose their operating schedules; there were no stringent attendance requirements, and individual school districts had the option to provide additional funds to extend the school year to four months or longer. County taxes supplemented public school funding. In fact, the early public school system was heavily dependent on county-level administration and planning, and often required private resources.

In 1841 there were more than twenty-five hundred public, or "common," schools statewide. The three-month session was increased to six months in 1860, and the number of school districts in Randolph increased to seventy-one with a school in each district, thereby making it possible for students to walk to school and providing each community with an identity and a gathering place. Men, many of them ministers, filled most of the teaching positions. The curriculum covered reading, writing, spelling, and arithmetic. At several schools the few available textbooks were often hand-copied for broader distribution. From the outset, Randolph County suffered from a severe shortage of teachers. This shortage became more acute when the number of school districts increased from the original twenty-one to seventy-one. The teacher shortage abated somewhat within a few years when "graduates" of the schools became teachers, but the problem worsened with the advent of the Civil War. With no compulsory attendance laws, many students missed school because of farm duties.

The Asheborough Female Academy, a private school, was constructed ca. 1839 on a one-acre lot downtown. During the Civil War, Confederate troops were sometimes billeted here. Photograph courtesy of the Randolph County Public Library.

A number of private schools existed during this era as well. These institutions struggled, with most operating on irregular schedules depending on the availability of teachers and funds. Noteworthy were the Asheborough Female Academy and the Asheborough Male Academy. Jonathan Worth, who had five daughters, was instrumental in organizing the Female Academy, which opened in 1839. The school prospered, and its advertisements in Fayetteville and Cheraw, South Carolina, newspapers touted Asheboro as a place "believed to be as healthy as any other in the United States." The school lacked a dormitory, so out-of-town girls boarded with local families, including the Worths who took in six girls. Other area academies established prior to 1860 included Middleton (est. 1841), near Franklinville, and Science Hill (est. 1845), in Concord Township. The number of female teachers in the county increased from one in 1853 to eleven two years later, compared to forty-nine male teachers in 1855.

Charlesanna Fox, the longtime librarian at the Randolph County Public Library and primary author and editor of *Randolph County, 1779-1979*, described Randolph citizens Jonathan Worth and Braxton Craven as "two of the most zealous friends of the common schools the state has ever had." Craven was the driving force behind

The Asheborough Female Academy, shown here in 1974, was restored to reflect its original condition. Photograph courtesy of the State Archives.

the development of Trinity College. The school, originally established as Brown's School in Trinity Township under the guidance of Brantley York, was renamed Union Institute in 1839 to denote a union between the five Quakers and twenty-two Methodists who had formed an association to develop a school with adequate facilities and a strong faculty. Craven became an assistant teacher under York in 1841 and later succeeded him. In 1851, Craven, aware of the general need for qualified teachers, changed the school's name to Normal College in the hope of attracting students desiring to become teachers. In 1859 Normal College became Trinity College. Craven's leadership and initiative made him a prominent figure in Randolph County before and during the upcoming Civil War.

Randolph County residents had achieved remarkable break-throughs in creating a new county and developing some of the area's resources within the span of three-quarters of a century. However, many challenges remained ahead, and individuals such as Braxton Craven and Jonathan Worth would help guide the county through the remainder of the nineteenth century.

CHAPTER THREE

Communities, Leaders, and Civil War

*W*ith the exception of Asheboro—sited because it lay at the geographical center of the county—other Randolph County towns arose for one of several reasons: they were located near water or other natural resources, trading paths or roads; or they served as settlements for those of the same religious faith.

In or around 1786, members of the Society of Friends migrated from Bush River in South Carolina to the northwestern corner of Randolph, thus augmenting the colony of Quakers across the border in Guilford County. They named their settlement Bush Hill (renamed Archdale in 1887). These new residents worshiped at Springfield Meeting with the Guilford County Quakers. The men were skilled wood and leather craftsmen and became known for their superior products. By 1825 in Bush Hill, Allen U. Tomlinson utilized steam to power a large tannery, which burned in 1845 but was rebuilt as Tomlinson, English, and Company. W. C. Petty, D. M. Petty, and Moses Hammond opened a business there around 1845 to make sashes, doors, and other

Allen U. Tomlinson owned a large tannery in Bush Hill (later Archdale). According to the Randolph County Public Library website, he proposed to representatives of the Confederate government that for every two pairs of shoes he made for the army, one Quaker man would not be drafted into the army. Photograph courtesy of the Randolph County Public Library.

building products. William Tomlinson's second son, Josiah Tomlinson, received a grant of three hundred acres when he arrived in the area and began making shoes, harnesses, horse collars, and saddles. Eli Haworth and family organized a company utilizing wagons to transport local products to market. The Quaker families who moved to Bush Hill intermarried with other Quakers who attended Springfield Meeting. Likewise, their business activities were with kinsmen, and this is reflected in the names of the companies they operated. At the onset of the Civil War, the Bush Hill community lost a number of families when many local Quakers, who opposed slavery and advocated emancipation, moved to Indiana.

The Archdale and Trinity communities have never had an easily distinguishable border, but they now share one in common: Archdale's western and Trinity's eastern. Whereas Archdale drew its citizens by industrial development, Trinity began as an agricultural community, and families tilled nearby parcels and lived in the village. The first settlers arrived prior to 1780, and within ten years there were approximately twenty-five families living in the Trinity area. Most of them were baptized into the Methodist Episcopal faith by circuit-riding evangelists. Residents organized Hopewell Methodist Episcopal Church in 1819. The community remained largely agrarian until the 1839 opening of the educational institution that later became Trinity College. Soon after the college's opening came a gradual influx of professional educators and businesses to support the college community. Some farmers became shopkeepers or entered other trades. These farming families eagerly welcomed Trinity College, many opening their homes to boarding students. The village grew, streets were laid out, and many families from Randolph and other counties relocated to Trinity to educate their sons and settle in this "fine community." As the college grew and thrived, Trinity residents prospered as well. In 1869 the town was chartered as Trinity College, and it consisted of a growing cluster of fine homes, many of which are still standing, including that of Dr. Stephen B. Weeks—one of the state's early historians—as well as homes of merchants, tradesmen, physicians, and teachers.

Randleman, another of Randolph's early settlements, traces its beginnings in 1800 to Peter Dicks's gristmill. At this time, the community was known as Dicks or Dicks Crossing because of its location at a ford on Deep River. By 1848 Union Factory had

This 1891 photograph shows Trinity College students in front of the school building. The wings, an addition to the original structure, are on the left. Photograph courtesy of the Randolph County Public Library.

opened, producing cotton cloth, and the community became known as "Union." John Banner Randleman and John H. Ferree purchased the factory in 1868 and changed its name to Randleman Manufacturing.

Nearby New Salem—a community that reached its peak in the nineteenth century—was first settled in the late 1700s and laid off in 1818. Located about two miles north of Randleman on the trading path, New Salem initially thrived but was isolated in the twentieth century because a major highway was constructed that bypassed the village. The town prospered for decades until the establishment of cotton mills and other industries offered employment elsewhere in the county. Many residents (including numerous Quakers) subsequently moved. The village's leading merchant, a Quaker named William Clark, relocated to Randleman to become the sales agent for Union Manufacturing Company. Later, owing to his antislavery beliefs and his fears of a developing national conflict, he moved his large family to Indiana.

Early New Salem enterprises included wool carding, a buggy and carriage shop, a general store and post office, a hotel and tavern, a tannery, a boot maker, and a tin shop. Benjamin Swaim, by far the town's most influential citizen, published a business periodical that he also compiled into a book. The compilation, entitled *The Man of Business*, provided instructions and advice on legal and business documents and procedures. The Society of Friends established New Salem Meeting in 1813, but because of a declining Quaker population the group sold the building to a Methodist Protestant group in 1885. New Salem Masonic Lodge, established in 1859, later moved to Randleman. Even after Randleman lured away many citizens and businesses, New Salem remained an educational center with an academy and a printing plant.

Liberty, in the northeast quadrant of Randolph County, traces its beginnings to 1815, when tax listings showed that a dozen taxables owned land in the midst of a thriving agricultural area. Southwest of Liberty lies the town of Franklinville. The town, incorporated in 1847 and named for former governor Jesse Franklin, received a new charter in 1848 in order to remove the "s" from the original name of Franklinsville. A post office opened there in 1840, about the same time that the Horney and Makepeace families established the Middleton Academy, a private school operated before the county school opened in 1845.

For decades after its chartering in 1796, Asheboro remained a sleepy little village, coming to life only when the county court convened; otherwise, there existed few activities or other compelling reasons for the area's rural residents to relocate to the town. General merchandise stores provided essentials for townspeople and neighboring farm families. Absent was a river to provide waterpower for industries and a railroad to convey products to market. The courthouse and general merchandise stores acted as Asheboro's only inducements.

In January 1840 Simeon Colton of Fayetteville, an agent of the North Carolina Board of Internal Improvements (and later pastor of Asheboro Presbyterian Church), attempted to interest investors in financing the construction of a railroad connecting the Piedmont area with Fayetteville. Randolph County's most prominent citizens— Gen. Alexander Gray, Congressman John Long Jr., county clerk Jesse Harper, Jonathan Worth, and Henry B. Elliott—published a notice in the *Asheboro Southern Citizen* calling for a meeting to identify potential investors in the proposed railroad. The meeting at the Randolph County Courthouse failed to provide sufficient impetus or to raise funds. Despite the ineffectiveness of this and other efforts to induce growth, on January 7, 1845, the General Assembly passed an act incorporating the town of Asheboro and appointing commissioners Jonathan Worth, Alfred Marsh, Hugh McCain, James M. A. Drake, and Hardy Brown. However, nearly a half century elapsed before Asheboro emerged as more than Randolph's county seat.

Meanwhile, as in other communities, local citizens established churches in Asheboro. Built in 1834, Asheboro Methodist Episcopal Church—now First United Methodist Church—was the town's first organized church. Asheboro Presbyterian Church followed in 1850. The first church for the town's African American worshipers was established in 1869 on South Fayetteville Street. Originally known as Bulla Grove, the church later relocated to Burns Street and took the name St. Luke's United Methodist.

Throughout Randolph County, at least twenty-five Methodist Episcopal and thirteen Methodist Protestant churches formed prior to the Civil War. The Christian denomination arose in 1782, created by dissenters from the Methodist Church. The Reverend Thomas C. Moffitt ultimately organized five Christian denomination churches: Shiloh, Christian Union, Pleasant Ridge, Pleasant Grove, and Parks Cross Roads Christian Churches, all of which survive. Other congregations formed as well. Randolph Friends established five new Quaker meetings, but only two survive today: Bethel and Cedar Square. Allen U. Tomlinson established the county's first "Bible school" in 1822 at Springfield Meeting, and it operated for four decades. After establishing themselves early, Baptists organized several new churches between 1800 and 1860. Welborn Chapel appeared in 1806, followed by Shady Grove (1836) and Cedar Falls (1844) Baptist Churches. Ramseur Baptist (1851) was that town's only church until 1886. *Branson's North Carolina Business Directory* of 1894 listed forty-five ministers in Randolph County. Many ministers served more than one church.

A number of Randolph County natives assumed leadership roles at both the state and national levels—and even in the Confederate Congress—during the eighteenth and nineteenth centuries, in addition to those answering the call to bear arms in combat.

Probably no Randolph citizen enjoyed a longer or more diversified period of public service than Alexander Gray, whom voters elected to fifteen sessions of the state senate between 1789 and 1831. Gray was one of the wealthiest men in the area, and his ownership of 118 slaves made him the largest individual slaveholder in either Randolph or Guilford County. His plantation occupied 2,190 acres located about five miles southwest of Trinity. After the death of his first wife, Gray married Sarah Harper Elison, daughter of Col. Jeduthan Harper. During the War of 1812, while serving in the state senate, Gray was appointed brigadier general (the first Randolphian to achieve that rank) and slated to command a brigade of the North Carolina militia. En route to assuming command, he received word that a treaty had been signed, thereby ending his military career before it had really begun.

Jonathan Worth was born November 18, 1802, to industrious, well-educated, and thrifty Quaker parents—Dr. David and Eunice Gardner Worth—in the Guilford County community of Centre Friends Meeting, now known as Centre, a short distance north of Randolph County. His father, a medical doctor, strongly espoused the Quakers' antislavery beliefs. The Quakers considered slavery a moral issue, opposed holding human beings in bondage, and drove the agenda of the Manumission Society, which advocated the granting of freedom to individual slaves by their masters and by legislation. Other Worth family members actively supported the Underground Railroad, the loosely structured network of whites and blacks that provided assistance and shelter to fugitive slaves escaping from the South. Jonathan and two of his brothers, Dr. John Milton Worth (1811-1900) and Joseph Addison Worth, married Presbyterian women. As punishment for marrying outside the unity of Friends, their names were stricken from the rolls of Centre Meeting. Jonathan and Milton (as John Milton was known) reared their families in the Asheboro Presbyterian Church. The two brothers, who remained active leaders and generous contributors, never became communing members of this church. Addison (as Joseph Addison was known) was a merchant in New Salem. Three of the brothers' sisters married Friends, and the sisters' and their husbands' disdain for slavery, plus the threat of the impending Civil War, impelled them to follow many fellow Friends to Indiana.

Worth attended prestigious Greensboro Academy prior to reading law under the most distinguished jurist in North Carolina, superior

Jonathan Worth, a native of Asheboro, is the only Randolph County resident who has served as governor of North Carolina. Photograph courtesy of the State Archives.

court judge Archibald DeBow Murphey of Orange County. On April 20, 1824, Jonathan married Martitia Daniel, a niece and ward of Judge Murphey. When Worth moved with his young wife to Asheboro in 1824 and presented his license to practice law, there was little indication that this twenty-two-year-old barrister had the potential to ascend to the governorship of North Carolina; however, voters would twice elect Worth governor during the turbulent Reconstruction era. During the mid-nineteenth century, the Worth family would become a force in the political and economic arenas, not only in the Piedmont but also in Fayetteville, Wilmington, and other areas in eastern North Carolina.

Worth faced daunting personal challenges early in his legal career. His family, which included four children born in the Worths' first five years of marriage, lived in poverty before Jonathan overcame a crisis of confidence that threatened to end his career, despite his credentials and apparent skills, which indicated he was a bright and intelligent young man and perhaps as capable as any other lawyer.

Jonathan Worth apparently suffered from a fear of public speaking, a fact Col. John Hill Wheeler addressed in his book of reminiscences, noting that Worth "had been often heard to remark that he would rather lose a fee than make a speech." Worth entered politics to gain visibility (for attracting clients), to strengthen his meager elocution skills, and to overcome his shyness. Area voters sent Worth to the House of Commons in 1830 and 1831, and he achieved prominence during a stormy debate over a resolution he sponsored that denounced nullification. The doctrine of nullification, a contentious issue in the early 1830s and one espoused by many leading southerners (especially in South Carolina), proclaimed the rights of sovereign states to nullify any federal laws they deemed unconstitutional—essentially a "states' rights" position. Ostensibly an

Gov. Jonathan Worth and his wife Martitia had one son and seven daughters, five of whom are pictured here. The sisters are not identified. Photograph courtesy of the State Archives.

argument against the provisions of several federal tariffs (that many southerners felt put the South at an economic disadvantage), the doctrine's fundamental (and unenumerated) objective actually had more to do with fears of the centralization of federal power, which, among other concerns, appeared to some to threaten the future of slavery. Worth temporarily withdrew from politics after his 1831 term, though probably not because of any contentiousness over nullification. He remained busy representing clients in courts of the circuit.

Dr. John Milton Worth, nine years younger than brother Jonathan, followed their father and became a physician, locating his practice in New Salem. In 1834 he married Sarah Dicks, daughter of a prosperous New Salem merchant. Milton soon abandoned his medical career and moved to Montgomery County to follow other pursuits. He served in the state senate from 1842 to 1848 before moving to Asheboro to become involved in general merchandising, farming, and gold mining. Jonathan partnered with him in most of these ventures. The brothers' other enterprises included a copper-mining operation in Virginia; the Cape Fear Steam Boat Company, which traveled between Wilmington and Fayetteville; the Carolina City Company (formed to buy stock in the Atlantic and North Carolina Railroad Company); and the Western Plank Road Company.

U.S. senator Sam J. Ervin Jr. (1896-1985) of Morganton, North Carolina, took great pride in tracing his legal genes to prominent Randolph County attorney, Reuben Wood (1750-1812). Up until 1806, Wood practiced law in virtually every superior court and county court of pleas and quarter sessions between Asheboro and Jonesboro, Tennessee. Although he and his half brother, Zebedee Wood, both served as delegates to the state constitutional convention in 1789, and occupied seats in the state house in 1791, Senator Ervin delighted in telling that his great-great-great-grandfather was a practicing attorney and not a politician.

In addition to those who have served in the state legislature, two Randolph County residents have served in the U.S. Congress: John Long Jr. of Long's Mill (1821-1829) and William Cicero Hammer of Asheboro (1921-1930). Long was born February 26, 1785, in Loudoun County, Virginia; his family moved about a decade later to a farm three miles north of Liberty. A Whig, he served in the state house from 1811 to 1812, in the state senate from 1814 to 1815, and then for four terms in the U.S. Congress. A National Republican prior to becoming a Whig, Long won recognition as a staunch advocate of a strong protective tariff. His five sons included James Long, an attorney and editor of the *Greensboro Patriot*; William J. Long, an attorney who lived in the family's original home, which remained standing in the twentieth century; and John Wesley Long, a medical doctor. William Cicero Hammer was born near Asheboro on March 24, 1865. In 1891, after graduating from the University of North Carolina, he was admitted to the bar. His varied career included stints as mayor of Asheboro, superintendent of public instruction in Randolph County, and for over forty years, owner and editor of the *Asheboro Courier*. He was elected to Congress as a Democrat in 1921, serving five terms until his death on September 26, 1930.

Although not residents of, or representing Randolph County by the time of their 1870s congressional terms, both William McKendree Robbins and James Madison Leach did trace their origins to the Trinity community. Robbins (1828-1905) became the first professor of mathematics at Trinity College before resigning to study law. In 1854, he was admitted to the bar and moved to Alabama. He joined the Confederate army and, after the war, relocated to Salisbury, North Carolina, whose electorate sent him to the state senate in 1868 and 1870. Voters later elected Robbins to the U.S. Congress for three terms, from 1873 to 1879.

James Madison Leach (1815-1891) attended the United States Military Academy until 1838, studied law under his brother, I. E. Leach, and was admitted to the bar in 1842. For thirty years he enjoyed a thriving practice in Lexington, North Carolina, occasionally practicing law in Randolph as well. A longtime trustee of Trinity College and a community advocate, he fought the eventual removal of the college to Durham.

Leach achieved wide renown as a powerful orator. A biographer described him this way: "He [could] speak two or three hours without hesitating for a word and keep his audience in an uproar of laughter with his wit and humor and fine mimicry." Leach was also known as an effective campaigner who never lost an election, a reputation that seems to be borne out by the many offices he held. He was a member of the state House of Commons for five consecutive sessions, from 1848 to 1858. During that time, in 1856, he served as a presidential elector for the American (Know-Nothing) Party's Fillmore-Donelson ticket. He entered the U.S. Congress in

47

James Madison Leach was born at the family homestead, Lansdowne, in Randolph County. Although opposed to secession, Leach quickly raised a company of men to fight for the South when he heard that President Abraham Lincoln had called on North Carolina for troops. He eventually became lieutenant colonel of the Twenty-first Regiment, North Carolina Troops. (Date unknown). Digital photograph from Prints and Photographs Division, Library of Congress, Washington, D.C.

1859 (to 1861) as the Opposition Party candidate (some sources say Whig). Soon came the Civil War and after a year in the Confederate army, Leach resigned and won a seat in the Confederate States Congress in both 1864 and 1865. In 1865 and 1866, voters elected Leach to the state senate, and from 1871 to 1875 he was back in the U.S. Congress, this time as a conservative Democrat. His final term of public service lasted from 1879 to 1880, once again as a state senator, in which capacity he assisted Dr. John Milton Worth, the state treasurer, in settling and adjusting North Carolina's debt.

For nearly fifty years in the middle of the nineteenth century, Marmaduke Swaim Robins enjoyed a position as the foremost attorney in Randolph County. Born August 31, 1827, he graduated from the University of North Carolina, studied law under Judge William H. Battle, and joined an existing law practice with Samuel S. Jackson (Jonathan Worth's son-in-law) in Asheboro. As captain of the Home Guard during the Civil War, he narrowly escaped death when ambushed by a deserter. Voters elected him to the state house in 1862, and for several months he acted as house Speaker. Robins returned to Raleigh four other times, serving in both the senate and house. He later held the positions of private secretary to Gov. Zebulon B. Vance and editor of the *Raleigh Conservative* newspaper.

During the mid-nineteenth century, several of Randolph County's more prominent leaders were newspaper publishers. In part because the county lacked a large or regionally prominent settlement, its first local newspaper debuted comparatively late—1836—nearly a century after the establishment of the state's first newspaper in New Bern. Benjamin Swaim published the *Southern Citizen* weekly from 1836 to 1844, operating for the first ten months in New Salem before moving to Asheboro. The *Christian Sun* weekly (1844-1900), an official organ of the Southern Christian Church, appeared next on the Asheboro scene, followed by the *Randolph Herald* (1846-1850) and the weekly *North Carolina Bulletin* (1856-1857). In May 1850, Braxton Craven and Reuben H. Brown, a native of Randolph County, began publishing *Southern Index* at Asheboro. The sixteen-page periodical, devoted primarily to promoting public education, also included a variety of subjects. In October 1850, it was renamed *Evergreen*. Craven continued with *Evergreen* until March 1851, when he relinquished his shares of the magazine to Brown. The venture survived until November 1851. A writer of articles on the social and economic relationship between the North and South, Craven published a number of short stories in these magazines. He wrote several works under the pseudonym Charlie Vernon, including two short novels: *Mary Barker*, published in the 1860s; and *The Story of Naomi Wise, or, The Wrongs of a Beautiful Girl*, in the 1880s.

As they neared the mid-1800s, residents of Randolph County had witnessed numerous developments and changes. Five cotton mills enhanced the local economy; the westward migration of Quakers and those seeking rich land in Ohio and Indiana had subsided; several gold mines prospered; roads and new modes of transportation developed; public schools expanded and improved; and several county leaders occupied prominent roles in state government. During the 1850s, sectional controversy and questions over the expansion of slavery took center stage in the national debate. However, these heated issues were of lesser importance to most Randolph residents, mainly because of the relative insignificance of slavery in the county, but also partly because of the county's isolation.

In 1780 the slave population in Randolph amounted to 7.3 percent of the overall population and increased to 10.7 percent by 1815. By 1850 the slave population stood at 10 percent in Randolph, compared with, in surrounding counties, 32 percent in Chatham, 26 percent in Montgomery, and 21 percent in Moore. The 1860 census indicated a Randolph County population of 16,793, consisting of 14,715 whites, 1,646 slaves, and 432 free blacks. Only 344 Randolph families or individuals owned slaves in 1860, and half of these owned only one or two. Only four citizens possessed more than thirty slaves, and these families ran comparatively extensive farming operations that required not only more field hands but also ancillary workers to maintain equipment, and wagon drivers to transport produce to market. These figures highlight the first of two important reasons for the county's low slave population: Randolph's predominant small family-operated farms raised crops not requiring extensive labor; and the sizable numbers of Quakers, Moravians, Dunkers, and Wesleyans (called "Abolition Methodists"), all of whom were opposed to slavery because of their religious and/or personal convictions. Consequently, several citizens worked to bring about emancipation.

On some small family-owned Randolph farms, the relationships between slaves and their owners differed markedly from those on eastern North Carolina plantations. Family members often worked side-by-side with the slaves. Gen. Alexander Gray, Randolph's largest slaveholder, held the first meeting of the county Manumission Society in 1817 in his barn, located in Trinity Township. Despite his dependence on slavery, he strongly advocated the gradual eman- cipation of all slaves. In 1857, Guilford County native Daniel Worth,

a cousin of Jonathan Worth, returned to North Carolina from Randolph County, Indiana, working as an Abolition Methodist missionary after having abandoned his Quaker upbringing.
He operated from his daughter and son-in-law's home in New Salem. Controversy immediately accompanied Daniel Worth. He accused the Friends of fostering the institution of slavery, and his diatribes provoked Quakers and the state's leading politicians. Even though Friends opposed slavery, they did not condone its condemnation from the pulpit. Authorities arrested Worth for sedition, and he later fled the state in order to escape a long-term prison sentence.

Beginning around 1840 and continuing into the years immediately preceding the Civil War, Braxton Craven and other faculty members at Trinity College decried the dependence of the South upon the North. Their writings contained fervent pleas for southern economic and intellectual development.

Trinity College served as a frequent forum for lectures and debates on slavery and the political and intellectual differences between the North and South. In an April 1860 public address, Craven discussed the conditions of "Southern Civilization" to demonstrate why he believed the South had become subject to the North, and he urged the South to arouse its energies:

In position we never have been free. The Revolution broke our servitude to England but left the South subject to the North. I am for the Union against all comers now and forever, but I am also for southern social independence. We have served our time as overseers, factors, and clerks; it is time to commence business on our own resources.

Craven (who lost his parents at age seven) was reared by Nathan Cox, a prosperous Quaker farmer, at his home four miles southeast of Ramseur. Despite this Quaker influence, Craven later became a Methodist and obtained a license to preach. Paradoxically, he owned two slaves.

Immediately preceding and during the Civil War years, western North Carolina (and to a lesser extent, the Piedmont) contained large numbers of Unionists. The Randolph area's pro-Union support dwindled somewhat after Confederate forces fired on Union-held Fort Sumter on April 12, 1861, in the opening salvos of the Civil

The Reverend Braxton Craven, an educator, editor, and writer, served as president of Trinity College prior to and during the Civil War. In his editorials he appealed for the South's economic and intellectual development. Photograph courtesy of the State Archives.

War, and after Gov. Henry T. Clark ordered that one-third of the militia be drafted to protect against invasion of the North Carolina coast. Arguably, owing to President Lincoln's decision to force the issue at Fort Sumter, by this time the majority of the state's leaders, newspaper editors, and residents supported secession. Jonathan Worth felt that Lincoln's actions forced North Carolina and other Upper South states with Unionist tendencies (such as Tennessee, Virginia, and Arkansas) to join the Confederacy. However, Worth expressed his reservations to a family member, stating, "I think the South is committing suicide, but my lot is cast with the South and being unable to manage the ship, I intend to face the breakers manfully and go down with my companions."

In Randolph there existed widespread support for the Union. Many residents felt they had no cause to fight for the Confederacy because they owned no slaves; others, having been loyal citizens of the Union all their lives, were convinced that fighting for the Confederate States of America was a lost cause. Many believed that the Confederacy could not win a war, especially because it had no standing army, no munitions and arms factories, and few sources for war supplies. For Quakers, war ran contrary to their religious belief against bearing arms. Those who fell into these various categories objected to being conscripted into the Confederate army because they had every intention of remaining neutral. But while some adamantly opposed the Confederacy, others endorsed its cause, believing they had no other option after the state seceded; still others hoped they would not have to make a choice. Jonathan Worth, for one, pledged his support to the new Confederate government by resigning his seat in the North Carolina Senate after both houses of the state assembly named him their choice for treasurer and Gov. Zebulon B. Vance appointed him to the position. Worth served as treasurer from 1862 until the end of hostilities.

A referendum on February 28, 1861—coming after seven of the eventual eleven Confederate states seceded, but before the war began—demonstrated the sentiments of citizens in the state and in Randolph. In this referendum, North Carolinians narrowly voted against holding a convention to consider secession from the Union— 47,373 to 46,672. Randolph County voters were, at this stage, overwhelmingly against secession, voting 2,446 against and only 45 for. Traditions of pacifism and antislavery had been instilled in many Randolph families for generations—not only those with strong religious beliefs and pacifist tendencies (such as Quakers), but also those yeomen of the soil who did not own slaves. Delegates at a subsequent state convention passed an ordinance of secession on May 20, 1861. The states bordering North Carolina to the south had already seceded, in effect spurring North Carolina to make a decision.

In April 1862, when the Confederate Congress passed a conscription law, anti-Confederate sentiment ballooned in Randolph among Quakers and others opposed to slavery, secession, and conscription. By the previous autumn, volunteering in the South had begun to taper off. Out of sheer necessity—in part because of a lack of sufficient reenlistments—the Confederate Congress instituted the conscription of white males between the ages of eighteen and thirty-five, subjecting them to the possibility of three years of service. (Exemptions allowed individuals in certain occupations, including those producing materials for the war, to avoid conscription.)

By 1864 the age ranges had been expanded twice, dashing the hopes of many in Randolph who had planned to remain neutral. Confederate officials experienced difficulty enforcing conscription, especially in more remote and rugged areas, including Randolph County. People were particularly aggravated that men of draft age owning twenty or more slaves enjoyed exemptions; this stipulation applied to virtually no one in the county, and residents viewed the law as favoring other regions.

Prior to October 1862, when legal measures became more stringent, Quakers were allowed exemptions from conscription by the state militia upon payment of one hundred dollars in gold or silver, and by the Confederacy upon remittance of five hundred dollars. Randolph's Isham Cox and other Quakers visited President Jefferson Davis and other Confederate leaders to present the Friends' pacifist position. The leaders received the delegation with dignity, but Quakers' hopes for exemption diminished when Davis expressed regret that there existed within the boundaries of the Confederacy a body of people unwilling to fight and, if necessary, to die in defense of their country. Reporting this incident in his book *Friends at Holly Spring*, Friends minister and historian Seth B. Hinshaw (Isham Cox was his great-uncle) stated that the Quaker delegation explained to Davis that, to them, their "country" meant "the United States," to which one of the Confederate officials present responded, "Doubtless your people [Quakers] are in the Northern Army fighting us; why should you not join us in fighting them?" Cox responded that he would be willing to oppose, single-handedly, "every *true* Friend in the Northern Army."

Centre Friends Meeting served as the home base of area abolitionists and the Manumission Society, whose purpose was to gain freedom for slaves. The Quaker-populated areas of central North Carolina served as the center of activity for the Manumission Society in the state. Many local Friends also were active supporters of the Underground Railroad. Although the "railroad" primarily served to shepherd blacks to freedom, it also aided draft dodgers and Unionists seeking to escape the Confederacy.

In the southern regions of Randolph, members of Holly Spring Meeting united in opposing war of any description. The historian Hinshaw wrote that "insofar as can be ascertained, no member of this meeting ever took a weapon into his hands." Some Quakers paid the exemption tax, and a few took jobs at the state saltworks near Wilmington, only to be exposed to yellow fever from the mosquito-infested swamps and to Union soldiers and bombardments from ships maintaining the Union blockade of Southern ports. Jonathan Worth's brother, Dr. John Milton Worth, became superintendent of the saltworks, an operation in which wood-fired boilers (which Worth purchased in Norfolk, Virginia) were filled with salt water taken from deep wells. Sixty gallons of salt water produced a barrel of salt, which the South needed for preserving pork and beef for the troops, for seasoning food, cooking, and curing leather. Union bombardments destroyed the Wilmington saltworks on Christmas Eve 1864.

While some Quakers and others seeking exemptions opted for employment at the saltworks, other men sought work in jobs that provided supplies for Confederate troops. One could find employment at one of five cotton mills on the falls along Deep River. These mills produced cotton fabric used for fashioning underwear and clothing. That these mills were small operations perhaps helped protect them from Gen. William T. Sherman's marauders, although the "bummers" did not venture far into the North Carolina Piedmont. The mills operated day and night to produce goods for the Confederacy, and Jonathan Worth spent much of his time searching for cotton (a scarce commodity in the Piedmont) to keep the mills busy. Most other local wartime manufacturing consisted of cottage industries operated by women, supplying troops with items ranging from tents to socks and hospital supplies. The women supporting these home-front operations suffered severe hardships because of shortages of food and other essentials. At war's end, North Carolina was the only Southern state whose men were not in rags because it had an agreement with the Confederacy to clothe, feed, and equip its own troops.

Tomlinson, English, and Company, a large tannery and shoe-manufacturing facility at Bush Hill (renamed Archdale in 1887), contracted with the Confederate army to furnish shoes, and this provided draft-exempt employment for some local men. The army contract stipulated that each employee produce a minimum of three pairs of shoes per day. Some expert craftsmen could make from six to eight pairs daily. Other potential draftees acquired exemptions to mine iron ore at the Franklinville smeltery and at Iron Mountain in Grant Township.

Quakers Thomas and Jacob Hinshaw, and Cyrus and Nathan Barker, brothers-in-law (the Barkers' sisters married the Hinshaw brothers), were among the Randolph Friends who, rather than seeking outside employment, opted to remain home and attempt to maintain normal lives by raising crops and caring for their families. In 1863 Confederate soldiers forcibly conscripted the four, tying them to gun carts and taking them to a militia camp near Buffalo Ford. The men were thrust into the Confederate army and often bodily harmed when they refused to carry out orders. Following the Battle of Gettysburg in July 1863—a battle in which the Hinshaws and Barkers refused to participate—the four were captured and suffered imprisonment at Fort Delaware, a Union prison located on an island in the Delaware River. Concerned Quakers in Wilmington, Delaware, and Philadelphia asked President Lincoln to free the men. Lincoln immediately issued an order granting the request, and Baltimore and Philadelphia Quakers helped ensure the men's safe arrival in Indiana where they joined relatives. In the autumn of 1864, when Mary Hinshaw and her sister, Elizabeth Hinshaw, learned of the whereabouts of their husbands, they loaded provisions and their four children into a covered wagon and traveled the six hundred miles from Randolph across the mountains to their new homes in Indiana.

Quakers like the Hinshaws and Barkers had been among the county's most ardent and active supporters of peace. A "Peace Meeting," partly in response to conscription, convened on March 12, 1862, at Scott's Old Field in Tabernacle Township. John C. Hill rallied attendees with a white flag, challenging those who supported the peace movement to fall in beside him. Some fifty men responded, demonstrating their support. As early as August 1861, similar demonstrations had taken place in the Franklinville and Foust's Mill areas.

A larger peace movement emerged in the South in the winter of 1863-1864, and was especially strong in North Carolina. The fall of Vicksburg, Mississippi, and the Confederate defeat at Gettysburg— provided impetus for the movement. William Woods Holden, editor of the Raleigh-based *North Carolina Standard* newspaper, served as

Quakers Thomas and Mary Hinshaw. (Date unknown). Photograph courtesy of the Randolph County Public Library.

the movement's leading advocate. Holden believed that by negotiating with the Union for peace, an independent Confederacy would result. In February 1864, at one of approximately one hundred peace meetings (mainly held in Piedmont and western counties), Holden received the Peace Party nomination for governor.

The election of 1864 further illustrated the views of the citizenry when Peace Party candidates received the majority of the votes in Randolph, one of only three counties in the state to support Holden for governor. The election of Zebulon B. Vance to the governorship essentially ended any possibility that North Carolina might leave the Confederacy. Vance had originally opposed secession, as did other state leaders—including Holden, John Motley Morehead, and Jonathan Worth—but he supported the Confederacy once North Carolina joined. Vance was not entirely uncritical of Confederate leadership, however, and voiced complaints about the Conscription Act of 1862.

Although many in the county avoided conscription, Randolph supplied soldiers for nine full Confederate army companies and half the troops for four more. Others dispersed to additional units. Many of these men fought in every battle in which the Army of Northern Virginia was involved, except First Manassas (called Bull Run in the North), the Civil War's first major engagement. Later, many Randolphians serving in the Confederate army deserted and returned home following the Battle of Gettysburg.

In northern Randolph at Trinity College, President Braxton Craven organized students and faculty into the Trinity Guard in May 1861. It was an effort to thwart the students from volunteering into the Confederate army. About forty students had volunteered at the end of the school year, and the remainder talked of volunteering or not returning to school for the next session. The Trinity Guard assisted in calming local disturbances. Gov. Henry T. Clark enlisted Craven and the unit to care for the first Union army prisoners confined at Salisbury, the site of the only major Confederate prison in North Carolina. During its existence the camp detained approximately fifteen thousand Union army prisoners, of whom more than four thousand died in captivity. Captain Craven and his student soldiers had been stationed there for only a few weeks when a major from Georgia assumed command and sent them back to Trinity. Craven's boys became draft-eligible after he unsuccessfully sought student exemptions.

Neither a battle nor a skirmish between Confederate and Union troops occurred in Randolph County during the Civil War. However, daily strife, mayhem, thievery, and destruction of property existed between neighbors, and even between family members, as citizens loyal to the Union joined draft dodgers and deserters to form an underground society of anti-Confederates that unleashed terror on the countryside. By the autumn of 1862, the informal merger of Unionists and deserters marked the coalescence of the anti-Confederate movement in the Randolph area. Occasionally the Home Guard (authorized by the state legislature and charged with enforcing the conscription laws, arresting deserters, and protecting pro-Confederate citizens from dissidents), Senior Guard, and Confederate army troops had to be summoned to capture or slow down the bands of armed men and send them scurrying back to their hideouts in the forests, hills, or caves. The area suffered from a shortage of available local men for controlling the somewhat chaotic situation in Randolph because even though the county had furnished some three thousand soldiers to the Confederacy, the soldiers served in units far from home.

The Trinity Guard was organized by Braxton Craven in 1861. Photograph courtesy of the Duke University Archives.

Randolph County's so-called "inner civil war" stemmed from widespread defiance and resistance to Confederate authority, sentiments shared by elements in the fringe areas of adjacent Davidson, Moore, and Montgomery Counties. The mountains and rough terrain of western Randolph made it easy and relatively safe for those opposed to the Confederacy to scour the countryside for food, clothing, and cash once their families had exhausted home supplies. Men who were forced into hiding to escape conscription were unable to raise crops to feed their families, a situation they shared with neighbors who were away fighting in the Confederate army.

From the autumn of 1862 until war's end in the spring of 1865, constant turmoil brewed between the pro-Union and the pro-Confederate factions in Randolph County. Hundreds of deserters and draft dodgers, both locals and outsiders, joined militant Unionists by forming into bands often numbering from twenty to a hundred men. These bands frequently outmaneuvered Confederate authority (usually Randolph Home Guard or Senior Guard) because the "outliers" knew every possible hiding place in their rugged domain. Outliers often ambushed "hunters" or Home Guard members sent to capture deserters and draft dodgers. The hunters retaliated, destroying property and physically abusing the men's families.

The coalition of pro-Union individuals—known variously as abolitionists, Lincolnites, Tories, or Unionists—did not regard themselves as outlaws, traitors, or criminals, despite the labels thrust upon them by supporters of the Confederacy. Rather, Randolph County's Unionists regarded themselves as patriotic Americans engaging in guerrilla warfare to combat secession. This Unionist coalition, at first consisting mainly of locals, primarily operated in southern Randolph County, which harbored them in deep forests, high hills, and rocky terrain. The many Union sympathizers in the surrounding countryside (including a significant number of African Americans), and in adjacent counties, bolstered and sustained the Unionist coalition. Supported by underground Unionists, these outliers initiated a response to the coercion and physical abuses heaped upon them and their families by the pro-Confederate faction. A system of warning signals, mutual protection, and dugout caves helped aid the outliers. Additionally, many members of the local Home Guard and Senior Guard, whom leaders dispatched to arrest the outliers or "recusant conscripts" (as draft dodgers were often called), felt sympathy for those defying the Confederacy. As the war continued, these draft dodgers were joined by Confederate army deserters, a group consisting of Randolph residents and outsiders. In the final days of the Civil War, a number of Union army deserters found their way to the area to join Randolphians in the "inner civil war." For many months near the end of the war, Confederate troops in Randolph and elsewhere were compelled to live off the land and subsist by plunder and pillage.

Armed clashes between deserters and Confederate soldiers occurred in Randolph and in nearby counties. On at least seven occasions, beginning in August 1861 and continuing until March 1865, Confederate troops or Home Guard units from outside Randolph had to be summoned in an effort to stem the vicious acts of guerrilla warfare. These acts included the malicious burning of homes and farms; theft of food, livestock, money, and anything of value; and physical assaults. As the war dragged on, desertions from the Confederate army increased to the point that the situation in Randolph became chaotic, as scores of men were killed, homes burned, and property destroyed. In March 1865 fifty deserters ransacked the home of Mrs. I. H. Foust, a widow, and her daughter Sallie. The men stole a thousand dollars in specie (coin), another thousand in Confederate bank notes, and some treasury notes. The deserters purportedly locked the two women in a room and departed after collecting all available food.

Many Randolph County pro-Confederates mistreated individuals who provided supplies and support to the outliers. A number of well-documented accounts exist of acts of mistreatment by the military upon Randolph civilians, especially upon the wives, children, and parents of outliers. Home Guard members often coerced parents to divulge where their sons were hiding. In one incident guardsmen reportedly placed the thumbs of an elderly mother between the lower rails of a fence and put crushing weight upon them. A Col. Alfred Pike confessed to the torture, for the purpose of extorting information, of the wife of William Owens of Moore County. Owens was the leader of a band of deserters who committed depredations against residents of Moore, Montgomery, and Randolph Counties. According to other reports, interrogators would affix rope around a woman's waist and dangle her from a tree limb in an attempt to force her to talk. One young woman reportedly gave birth to a dead fetus after such inhumane treatment.

The above incidents, along with other instances of reported abuse and disorder, provoked Dr. John Milton Worth to persuade Gov. Zebulon Vance to offer amnesty to some of the "better class of deserters and recusant conscripts" (those not guilty of capital felonies) to help locate and capture "some of the robbers." A month later, in February 1865, the desperate governor persuaded Gen. Robert E. Lee to send a detachment of Confederate troops to Randolph to restore law and order. Lee responded by sending Milton Worth's son-in-law, Lt. Col. Alexander Cary McAlister (who had distinguished himself in combat), and six hundred regular troops to Randolph, Moore, and Montgomery Counties. These soldiers dispatched to Randolph were pulled from their entrenched positions around Petersburg, Virginia. McAlister received orders to arrest and detain deserters and to secure the services of persons who might guide his men to deserters' hideouts. The soldiers' additional duties consisted of protecting the bridges, warehouses, and rail lines under threat by General Sherman's movement from the south. Reports indicated that as many as six hundred deserters, from both Confederate and Union units, had fled to Randolph County. McAlister's men took into custody approximately one hundred of these deserters.

The most successful foray of McAlister's troops occurred in the southeastern section of the county, where the old Fayetteville and Western Plank Road (later N.C. 705) entered Randolph from Moore County. The March 1865 capture took place near Page's tollhouse, located near Gollihorn Spring and the residence of magistrate William Gollihorn. Gollihorn had been indicted for harboring his sons, Milton and Alpheus, and other deserters. Milton escaped, but Alpheus and Pvt. William F. Walters, a deserter from the Indiana cavalry, could not avoid capture. Among other atrocities attributed to Alpheus Gollihorn and Walters, the two stood accused of murdering John Vanderford, a Confederate soldier on convalescent leave, whom the men reportedly stripped of his clothing and valuables and shot dead on a road near the Gollihorn's residence. After McAlister's troops captured the two, Alpheus was executed by firing squad at the troop headquarters near Gollihorn Spring. A court-martial in Asheboro found Walters guilty, and he was shot. Superiors later ordered McAlister and his men to Salisbury to confront Stoneman's Raiders. Tennessee-based Union general George Stoneman had led a band of soldiers, his so-called "raiders," on a march through portions of North Carolina's Mountain and Piedmont regions, passing through and damaging several towns, including Salisbury, which Stoneman occupied on April 12, 1865. On this march his raiders destroyed bridges, factories, military supplies, railroads, and other public and private property.

Whereas the Gollihorn family avoided conscription and opposed Confederate operations, the nearby Page family displayed their loyalty to the Confederacy. Page's tollhouse on the plank road sat not far from the Gollihorn residence. James Page, the person employed to collect tolls, went to Richmond, Virginia, to serve as the doorkeeper for the house of the Confederate Congress. Back at home, his wife, Martha Shamburger Page, ran the toll operation, along with supervising twelve slaves and caring for five young children. She also received and dispersed reports from those on the stagecoaches traveling the toll road and often was the bearer of death messages to families.

Union general George Stoneman's raid into North Carolina and Virginia lasted from March 20 to April 23, 1865, and was made up of 4,000 cavalry and a battery of artillery. Stoneman's Raid was designed to assist Sherman's Carolinas Campaign by ruining the states' infrastructures through burning government property, destroying railroad tracks, and disrupting Confederate authority. Photograph courtesy of the State Archives.

Whatever their politics, local residents had to concern themselves with the possibility of plunder and attack, from enemies either real or perceived. Such was the case near the war's end when a small detachment of Union general William T. Sherman's soldiers made camp on the grounds of Asheboro Presbyterian Church, located across the street from the future site of the courthouse complex. Asheboro merchant W. H. Moring Sr. decided to share honey and onions from his nearby garden with the ranking Yankee captain. This act of sharing possibly saved Moring's home and his most valuable possessions, which were hidden above his living room ceiling.

A very clear threat materialized on April 16, 1865, when three brigades of Confederate general Joseph E. Johnston's troops—tired, ragged, hungry, and demoralized—arrived at the Red Cross section of the county, near Trinity. The Confederate soldiers had retreated from Sherman's army, which they had engaged east of Raleigh at the Battle of Bentonville on March 19-21. The soldiers camped at Red Cross for several days and terrorized the residents, taking what supplies they needed while foraging for survival. (Such activities had increased, in part, because of Gen. Robert E. Lee's surrender to Gen. Ulysses S. Grant a week earlier at Appomattox Courthouse; Lee's surrender had effectively signaled the end of the war.) Soon after, General Johnston reached a final surrender agreement with General Sherman on April 26 at the Bennitt farm (also known as Bennett Place) in present-day Durham County, officially bringing the war to an end in North Carolina. Sporadic fighting continued for another two weeks in the western part of the state. On May 2, Johnston's three brigades marched to Bush Hill and were mustered

This undated photograph shows minié balls found at the Bethel Methodist Protestant Church campground in Red Cross where Confederate soldiers had camped and foraged for survival. Photograph courtesy of the Randolph County Public Library.

out, with all men, regardless of rank, granted a Mexican silver dollar and twenty-five cents in U.S. silver.

Despite six military operations mounted against deserters, draft dodgers, and Unionists between July 1861 and March 1865, the campaign in Randolph against outliers was largely ineffective. Although exact numbers are unknown, more than one hundred may have been killed by pro-Confederate forces and the military. After the end of hostilities, deserters and others in hiding were free to come out into the open. A number of local Unionists and pro-Confederates sought revenge upon one another in physical attacks, but the majority apparently allowed the courts to settle grudges and disputes. Old wounds would take years to heal—psychological and physical wounds caused by bitterness, physical abuse, thievery, deprivation, and deceit by neighbor upon neighbor during the war years.

The end of the Civil War also brought forth another period of migration for a number of Randolph families—mostly Quakers and Unionists—who sought to start anew and to find more fertile land. Many joined relatives in Indiana or other midwestern states. This marked the continuation of a trend that had begun in the early nineteenth century and peaked in the late 1830s.

CHAPTER FOUR

From Reconstruction to the Close of the Nineteenth Century

$\mathscr{A}$s the war wound down, a group of conservative leaders persuaded Jonathan Worth to become a candidate for governor in the election of 1865, opposing W. W. Holden, the Peace Party candidate favoring a quick return to the Union. President Andrew Johnson (a North Carolina native) had earlier appointed Holden provisional governor under Johnson's program of presidential Reconstruction, a plan he referred to as "Restoration." The presidential program appeared lenient compared to the subsequent, and often-labeled "radical," congressional Reconstruction, which imposed more stringent requirements on the ex-Confederate states. Worth won by nearly six thousand votes, but Holden supporters elected a majority in the General Assembly and seven state congressmen.

Worth, who had served as state treasurer from 1862 to 1865 under Gov. Zebulon Vance, took over the governorship when the provisional government disbanded on December 28, 1865. He was reelected in 1866, again by a large majority, over Holden. Among the many problems and issues Worth faced as governor was the question of the future of ex-slaves freed upon the ratification of the Thirteenth Amendment. The first Reconstruction Act, passed in 1867 despite Johnson's veto, ushered in a decade of more "radical" policies, including North Carolina's installation into the federal Second Military District. In June of the next year, North Carolina met the standards for regaining representation in Congress; the state gained full readmission to the Union in July. However, Governor Worth was forced from office near the end of his second term on July 1, 1868, protesting when Gen. E. R. S. Canby, military general for North and South Carolina, under authority from Congress, moved up the date of governor-elect Holden's installation.

Tombstone of Jonathan Worth located in Oakwood Cemetery, Raleigh, North Carolina. Photograph courtesy of the Historical Publications Section.

President Johnson had initially expressed disappointment with Worth's election to office in 1865, but he later recognized that Worth possessed a true and conscientious desire to restore the Union. However, back home, Worth faced vicious verbal attacks by pro-Union adherents, who deemed him a "tool of the Secession Party." Governor Worth had failed to carry Randolph County in either gubernatorial election, and when he finally left public office in 1868, he was a man broken in spirit as well as health, which had deteriorated rapidly after years of long hours, disappointments, and stress. He died at his Raleigh home on September 5, 1869, and was buried in nearby Oakwood Cemetery. The epitaph above his grave reads, "Legislator, chief financial officer and governor of his native State. Faithful in All."

During Worth's years of public service, he had proven himself an ardent advocate of public education. In 1865, after the position of state superintendent of schools had been abolished, former superintendent Calvin H. Wiley and Worth fought the legislature to protect the school system, but legislative authority was greatly restricted because of pressure from the military Reconstruction government. The school law enacted in 1866 provided little more than funds sufficient for the maintenance of school buildings. The new North Carolina Constitution of 1868, enacted the year Worth left public office, strongly encouraged education, dictating that it be provided for both whites and blacks. Other educational measures that were stipulated in the constitution included the election of a secretary of public education, a general and uniform system of free public schools for all children between the ages of six and eighteen, a requirement for county commissioners to provide one or more public schools in each district, and additional school funding derived from fines and other sources. Nevertheless, progress in educating the masses proved slow, and during this era many children were not schooled.

Because of the modest progress in public education, some outstanding private academies arose in Randolph County after the Civil War. Among them were Farmer Academy, Shiloh Academy, and Why Not Academy; the latter, located in the community of Why Not, offered an extensive curriculum of businesses courses. Academies began disappearing once public high schools arrived, but for many years the academies trained scores of public school teachers and provided courses for students seeking an education beyond the four basics taught in the common schools: typically algebra, Latin, and geometry, plus perhaps a course in business.

The Asheborough Female Academy, shut down during the war, permanently closed a few years later. The Asheborough Male Academy, a three-room wooden structure that opened in 1839, also closed during the war years. It reopened in 1890 as Asheboro Graded School, which the public school committee purchased in 1891. The most learned and accomplished principal at the Male Academy reportedly was Dr. Simeon Colton, formerly of Fayetteville, a graduate of Yale, and pastor of the Asheboro Presbyterian Church. His wife held the headmistress position at the Female Academy.

Public schools were a bit more successful at remaining open during the war. In the early 1860s the number of female teachers in public schools increased to 50 percent in order to fill positions vacated by males. The Literary Fund used to establish common schools provided little assistance, however, for salaries or other educational needs.

The Civil War left North Carolina in dire economic straits, particularly for educational funding. Immediately afterward, school appropriations dwindled to only one hundred thousand dollars per year statewide—small compensation for the loss of the Literary Fund, the resources of which were reallocated to other projects—and it would be a decade before the most basic educational needs were met. In 1877 the legislature made compulsory, rather than permissive, the levying of county taxes for education. The state set up schools in separate districts for African American students. Some of the ex-slaves left Randolph County, but most remained, many working in the public sector and/or as sharecroppers, with landowners furnishing acreage, tools, seed, fertilizer, housing, and other essentials. After a sharecropper paid for services provided by the landowner, the two parties divided the harvests according to prior agreement.

After the war, schools received aid from several sources, including the Freedmen's Bureau, which helped build schools for black and white students in the districts of the Quaker-populated areas of Randolph and eight other North Carolina counties. The Baltimore Association of Friends maintained separate black and white schools in Randolph, Guilford, Alamance, and six other counties. William E. Mead, a Quaker from Brooklyn, New York, came to Asheboro and served in the 1880s as principal of the town's African American school, named Asheboro Academy. In addition to his work as a dedicated teacher and administrator, Mead was a talented musician, and he trained many students in concert bands that received widespread acclaim and acceptance among both the races. Mead also trained white musicians and served as pianist and organist at Asheboro Presbyterian Church, which caused some grumbling among the black population, a factor in Mead's decision to return to the North.

Financial aid for education came from several private sources, including the American Missionary Association. Northern benevolent organizations supplied teachers and buildings, and donated two dollars for every dollar raised locally. A unique teaching enterprise opened at Springfield, straddling the Guilford-Randolph border, where the Baltimore Friends established a model farm to teach farmers new and improved farming and animal husbandry techniques.

Although the local public school system continued to expand through the end of the century, Randolph County lost its only institution of higher education because of a March 20, 1890, decision. In a Durham meeting of the Trinity College board of trustees, the school accepted an offer of eighty-five thousand dollars from Washington Duke—founder of American Tobacco Company, and sixty acres of land from Julian S. Carr—capitalist, manufacturer, and philanthropist, to move the campus to Durham. The trustees' decision nullified an earlier commitment to move the college to Raleigh. The school actually moved in 1892 and later became Duke University.

Randolphians undoubtedly felt ready to move beyond the devastation of the Civil War and concentrate on the years ahead. In addition to building more schools, residents focused on further development in Randolph County, as towns and villages gained population and prominence. Moreover, with the establishment of new industries (notably hosiery mills and a bobbin factory), the emergence of a spirited and politically motivated newspaper competition, and the 1889 arrival of the railroad, the county seat of Asheboro slowly developed into more than just a tranquil little courthouse village.

The Southern Reconstruction era, and the decade following, constituted a period of emergence and growth for a number of Randolph County communities. Bush Hill received a municipal charter in 1874. Three years later, Quaker leaders renamed it Archdale, honoring a fellow Friend, colonial governor John Archdale. Local officials allowed the charter to lapse about 1924, and after the failure of a vote to merge Archdale with Trinity, Archdale citizens opted to get a new charter.

With no waterpower for industry, Liberty blossomed only after the arrival of the Cape Fear and Yadkin Valley Railway in 1884. The Liberty Academy opened its doors in 1885. Eleven years later it was renamed Normal College, largely serving as a teachers' school until burning down in 1907. The town suffered two devastating fires—

one in 1888 and the second in 1895—that destroyed much of the old town square. The Liberty Picker-Stick and Novelty Company (established 1910) was the town's first industry, later taking the name Liberty Furniture Company. After electricity arrived, the number of industries increased, with additional furniture, textile, and hosiery plants. The town, incorporated in 1889, had 636 residents in 1920.

South of Liberty is the town of Staley, originally known as Staleyville. Located on the land of Col. John W. Staley, a Confederate veteran whose 350 acres lay near the route of the Cape Fear and Yadkin Valley Railway, the town occupied a logical site for a depot. The depot served as the origination point for shipping lumber and cotton goods from factories in the nearby town of Ramseur. In 1889 the Staley Cotton Mill was chartered, but the operation moved to Siler City, in Chatham County, in 1895. The Staley Hosiery Mill operated from 1918 until its destruction by a tornado in 1954. The Carolina Pyrophyllite Mining Company ceased operations in 1956, but several furniture plants remained in Staley.

Southwest of Staley is Ramseur, a community that came alive in 1850 with the establishment of Deep River Mills. Upon the mill's 1879 purchase by W. H. Watkins, A. W. E. Capel, J. S. Spencer, Joseph McLauchlin, John H. Ferree, Elizabeth Coggins, and Miss A. Coggins, the new owners renamed the company Columbia Manufacturing. The town, known until then as Allen's Fall, was also christened "Columbia," then renamed "Ramseur" after Watkins suggested it in honor of his Civil War commander, Maj. Gen. Stephen D. Ramseur of Lincolnton, North Carolina. By 1884 the mill had twenty-eight hundred spindles and produced fourteen hundred pounds of yarn per month, its fifty employees earning an average of $16.50 per month. The mill also operated a cotton gin. The same owners organized Alberta Chair Company in 1889 to make chairs whose cane bottoms were crafted by employees at their homes. The chair factory burned around the turn of the twentieth century; the fire also destroyed Ramseur Broom Company, which later relocated to a new site in the county. The Cape Fear and Yadkin Valley Railway built a spur line to Ramseur in 1890, leading to further development, and by 1900 Ramseur had a lively business district; featured Baptist, Methodist Episcopal, and Christian churches; and was the third largest town in the county

Yow's Mill, a gristmill in Richland Township on the Moore County border, was established in 1820. A sawmill was added in 1870 and a turbine waterwheel installed about 1890. The gristmill shown here, now a crafts shop, was built about the turn of the twentieth century on the same site as the original. It retains an iron overshot waterwheel and milling equipment, in addition to the stone dam. Photograph by the author.

exceeded only by Randleman and Asheboro. Along the way, in 1892, male residents organized Marietta Masonic Lodge #444.

Located just west of Ramseur is Franklinville. Its first industry was a gristmill built in 1801 by Christian Morris, who sold it to Elisha Coffin in 1820. The town's two cotton mills stood in a state of disrepair after the Civil War, but new owners reorganized them, and within a few years the mills were prospering. By 1880, Franklinville contained sixty-eight households and a population of 366, which included millers, physicians, a cabinetmaker, a watchmaker, and a teacher. Until train service came to Franklinville and Staley in 1890, wagons shipped products from the towns' mills to Greensboro. The roller mill and textile plants in Franklinville changed hands again on March 31, 1923, this time to be operated by John Washington Clark. After his death in April 1969, his son, Walter M. Clark, took over. The operations later declared bankruptcy.

Not until 1883 did Asheboro citizens elect a mayor and town commissioners, empowered by an act passed on March 3 that also set the town's corporate limits. It had taken a century for Asheboro to total five hundred inhabitants, whereas Randleman, incorporated as

A group of picnickers, some holding fishing poles, poses at Naomi Falls Dam around 1910. A note at the bottom of the photo reads, "WHERE NAOMI WISE WAS DROWNED NAOMI FALLS, NC." The Naomi name is perpetuated in a popular folk ballad narrating the tragedy of the pregnant Naomi Wise, whom her lover, Jonathan Lewis, purportedly drowned in 1808. Lewis had spirited her away, crossing Deep River on the pretense of taking her to a preacher to be married. Her tombstone, pictured below, is in the Providence Friends Meeting Cemetery. Photographs courtesy of the Randolph County Public Library.

Randleman Mills in 1880, grew into a bustling town by attracting residents to work in the cotton mills and other industries clustered along Deep River. At one point, Randleman annexed the site of the cotton manufacturing plant at Naomi Falls, plus its surrounding village. The census of 1890 listed a Randleman population three times that of Asheboro, and by 1900, it was home to twenty-two hundred residents.

In his *Reminiscences of Randolph County,* attorney and historian

J. A. Blair wrote of Asheboro in 1876, "this quiet country village, encircled by the hills of pine, in unpretentious simplicity, has stood for a hundred years, without assuming an air of town life, unaffiliated by burglars, tramps, or insurance agents, in the enjoyment of the greatest earthly treasures, contentment and health." Sidney Swaim Robins, a doctor of philosophy, author, and college professor born in Asheboro in 1883, related many of his memories of the town just prior to and after the turn of the twentieth century in his book, *Sketches of My Asheboro: Asheboro, North Carolina, 1880-1910*. He spent much of his boyhood around the courthouse, which was the focal point of the community. Here is an excerpt from his book:

Around the courthouse was that square, which was often a noisy and riotous place, especially on Tuesday of the first week of court. We long had two court sessions a year, middle of July and in December. The first week was always given to criminal cases, and the second one was roughly reserved for the Civil Docket. The judge often had to call a halt in the proceedings of a trial and order the sheriff to go down and restore order and quiet around the building. The noises arose from horse-traders, vendors of patent-medicines, shillabers for peep shows and the like, and lastly from quarrelers and battlers likely stimulated by country brands of raw John Barleycorn. Many of these hawkers moved from one Court to another, and, in Asheboro at least, Tuesday was sure to be the big day. They camped oftentimes by open fires alongside their wagon-tongues, and slept in their wagons. This was also the way with some witnesses and principals to appear in court.

There were a lot of horse-traders around on Tuesday of Court, and somehow they seemed to make more noise than anybody else. Of course the animals themselves helped some. And showing off horses in crowds is noisy business. In July particularly, with windows open, it often sounded like Bedlam out there.

One of the county's last-established towns, Seagrove, did not exist prior to the arrival of the railroad and a post office in 1897. The emerging village's namesake, Edwin G. Seagroves, worked as the Aberdeen and Asheboro Railroad's construction engineer. From 1890 to 1930, Seagrove achieved notice as the "crosstie capital of the world." Seagrove citizens decided it appropriate to incorporate as a town in 1913, despite a population of only forty-one taxable residents. Within seven years the population increased to 189.

This Randolph County Courthouse, 1835-1909, was located in the middle of the intersection of Salisbury and Main Streets. It was the center of much activity on court day. Photograph courtesy of the Randolph County Public Library.

Seagrove Lumber, for many years the town's largest employer, began as Auman Lumber in 1926.

At the same time Randolph's towns were growing, notable individuals were developing enterprises, properties, and residential areas. One such locally prominent individual was W. Gould Brokaw, a wealthy New Yorker and grandson of railroad tycoon Jay Gould. In the 1890s Brokaw developed Fairway Park, a hunting estate comprised of the fifteen-bedroom Manor House, game preserves, polo field, swimming pool, squash courts, racetrack, and other amenities. Manor House lay about four miles south of Trinity and the nearest post office. Brokaw purchased twenty-three hundred acres for game hunting and leased thirty thousand more from adjacent property owners. Developing the estate required fifteen years, at a cost of a half-million dollars. Manor House attracted the wealthy and the famous, including the young Franklin D. Roosevelt, who visited about 1908, shortly after he received his law degree. An avid quail hunter, Roosevelt eagerly accepted an invitation to hunt on the Brokaw estate, which was well stocked with quail, pheasant, and wild turkey. After Manor House burned in 1922, the owner abandoned the other buildings, and they rapidly deteriorated. By the late 1920s Brokaw had sold the entire property.

Arguably the county's most prominent citizen during the mid- to late 1800s, Marmaduke Robins returned to Asheboro after completing his legislative and newspaper pursuits in Raleigh. He and his wife, Annie Eliza Moring Robins, had three sons, including Henry Moring Robins, who followed his father in the legal profession and served as Asheboro mayor, and the previously mentioned Sidney Swaim Robins, author of *Sketches of My Asheboro*, who became a professor of philosophy at Saint Lawrence University in Canton, New York. Marmaduke Swaim Robins founded the conservative *Randolph Regulator* on February 2, 1876, in order to counteract the influence of a Republican newspaper published in Greensboro and widely circulated in Randolph County. In 1879, seeking to escape the ridicule created by comparisons of his paper to a similarly named popular patent medicine, Robins changed the name to *Asheboro Courier,* and shortly thereafter sold the newspaper to J. T. Croker. Asheboro had two competing newspapers in 1879: the one directed by Robins, a staunch Democrat, and the *Randolph Sun*, edited by Republican J. A. Blair. Blair tired of the fray and discontinued his newspaper after thirty-three issues. But it proved a short vacation—

he and his brother soon thereafter founded the *Randolph Argus*, with J. A. as editor. The *Randolph Argus* closed after fire destroyed the newspaper's office on December 30, 1895. The *Asheboro Courier* changed hands several times until 1892, when Wiley Rush and William Cicero Hammer, two attorneys, became the owners. Rush later sold his interest. A third publication, the short-lived *Liberty Register*, circulated from 1898 to 1900.

William Penn Wood, an Asheboro merchant and Civil War veteran, holds the distinction of being the only Randolphian to win four consecutive terms as an elected state official. A Democrat, Wood served as state auditor from 1910 to 1920. At age eighteen Wood enlisted in the Confederate army. In 1873 he established the W. P. Wood Company, a general merchandise store that later merged with the store of W. H. Moring, the father of Annie Robins. Wood served as Asheboro city treasurer (1880-1888), as treasurer of

A view of Depot Street (now Sunset Avenue) in downtown Asheboro at about the turn of the twentieth century. The Bank of Randolph is at the end of the street, and the Wood & Moring general merchandise store is on the right, with the "WO" portion of the sign visible. The telephone poles and wires were installed about 1897 and the power poles about 1900. Photograph courtesy of the Asheboro Public Library.

Randolph County (1890-1894), as state senator (1901-1904), and as state representative (1905-1908).

Many members of Gov. Jonathan Worth's immediate and extended family stood among Randolph County's notables. Elvira Worth Jackson Walker Moffitt, Governor Worth's daughter, outlived three husbands and was a familiar figure in North Carolina and Virginia during her ninety-four years. She served as state regent of the Daughters of the American Revolution from 1906 to 1910; the organization later bestowed Moffitt with the title, Honorary Regent for Life. She also acted as honorary president of the United Daughters of the Confederacy, led a statewide movement to have a Confederate monument erected in every county, and strongly advocated historical preservation. Herbert Worth Jackson, her only child, became president of the Virginia Trust Company of Richmond, one of the first trust companies in Virginia and among the first in the South. Jonathan Worth's sister, Ruth Worth Porter of Greensboro, was the grandmother of the renowned author William Sydney Porter, better known as O. Henry. Joseph Addison Worth, the younger brother of Jonathan and John Milton, worked as a merchant and general agent for the Cape Fear Steam Boat Company. Many people regarded him as the most important businessman in Fayetteville during the Civil War.

Lt. Col. Alexander Cary McAlister (1837-1916), who married Dr. Milton Worth's daughter Adelaide, is perhaps best remembered as the man whom Gen. Robert E. Lee dispatched to round up the deserters and draft dodgers terrorizing Randolph County during the Civil War. The *Presbyterian Standard*, in a memorial on January 3, 1917, described McAlister as "first of all a citizen of the highest type. He took an active part in politics because he considered it the part of good citizenship." McAlister was a graduate of the University of North Carolina, chairman of the Randolph Board of Education, a member of the State Board of Public Charities, and an elder and clerk of session at Asheboro Presbyterian Church. He also served for a quarter century as chairman of the Democratic Party's county executive committee; he never ran for public office.

Alexander and Adelaide McAlister had six children. Their son Alexander Worth McAlister (1862-1946) was a prime force in transforming the village of Greensboro into a city. Instrumental in founding Pilot Life Insurance and four other insurance companies, he also developed the fashionable Irving Park residential community and helped establish the Greensboro and Sedgefield Country Clubs. In 1903, as vice-president of the insurance companies, Worth (as he was known) directed construction of the five-story Southern Trust skyscraper—at that time the tallest in the state. During World War I he served as the state fuel administrator. (The McAlister surname has since been altered by some descendants to "McAllister," with an additional "l.")

During the latter 1800s, the growing textile industry helped nurture new enterprises. The woodlands of Randolph County proved a prime source for construction materials and natural resources used by various industries. In 1867 Capt. William H. Snow, a Vermont native then living in Archdale, sold and shipped a barrel of persimmon shuttle blocks to a company in Lowell, Massachusetts, located in the heart of the textile industry. He charged a lower price than northern mills ordinarily paid for shuttle blocks derived from apple wood, thus creating a new market for local wood products. By 1884 shuttle block plants were operating in Central Falls and Archdale, as well as in Guilford County. Randolph's rich woodlands also prompted the founding of Snow Lumber, which furnished wood for furniture plants and the construction trade.

The furniture industry grew in part because it manufactured a product needed in the textile industry: the wooden spools or bobbins used to wind thread. Initially these items, plus shuttles and shuttle blocks, were acquired from firms in New England, where cotton mills proliferated. Later, these items were made in either small carpentry shops or in a mill's machine shop. As the number of cotton mills and looms increased in the Piedmont, more local sources for these wood products were needed. An early bobbin factory was that of A. G. Jennings and J. W. Tippett, who operated the Cedar Falls Bobbin Company as early as 1863. Seven years later the plant produced thirteen thousand bobbins, fifty bedsteads, and twenty-five bureaus, using waterpower to turn lathes. In 1900 W. A. Ward and

J. A. Martin opened Novelty Wood Works in Ramseur to make bobbins and picker sticks for cotton mills.[*]

The lean years of Reconstruction also spawned a renewed interest in gold mining, which at its peak consisted of at least seventy-eight sites in Randolph County. The quest for gold had started in the 1820s at placer mines, with many farmers panning the streams in the southwestern part of Randolph—the best means for a farmer to earn additional money after crops were harvested. The most successful early mines lay in the western part of the county. The best known and most profitable one, Hoover Hill Mine, commenced operations in 1848 in Tabernacle Township, located southwest of Randleman, near the Uwharrie River. It produced some seventeen thousand ounces of gold during its existence, but was abandoned in the early 1900s when the quantity and quality of its gold rendered it unprofitable. The operation covered approximately 250 acres, and a village sprang up around it, with housing, a commissary, and a blacksmith shop to repair the extensive conveyor equipment and pumps used in the shafts. A British company purchased the land and gold rights from Joseph Hoover in 1851 for $20,000. It formed a local company with a capital stock of $350,000. The mine employed a large force of Welsh and English miners as well as locals, and in its heyday paid monthly wages totaling approximately $12,000, at that time the largest payroll in the county.

In 1886 gold fever attracted to Asheboro three retired British army captains with the melodious names Charles St. George Winn, C. Slingsley Wainman, and Basil J. Fisher. The men—who sported knickers and caps, owned fast horses, built fancy and elaborate homes, and purchased considerable real estate—captured the imaginations of the villagers and engendered gossip over their activities. Winn, a hard-drinking bachelor, did not last long, reportedly dying in a bellowing fit of delirium tremens. Wainman built the first rental houses in Asheboro, and he, too, died within a few years. Fisher, the wealthier of the three, built a palatial home on Sunset Avenue, and after acknowledging gold to be less profitable than expected, engaged in other business enterprises. He later moved to Greensboro and developed the fashionable Fisher Park neighborhood. In 1919 his Sunset Avenue home was converted into Asheboro's second hospital.

[*] Shuttles, shuttle blocks, and picker sticks are parts of a weaving loom.

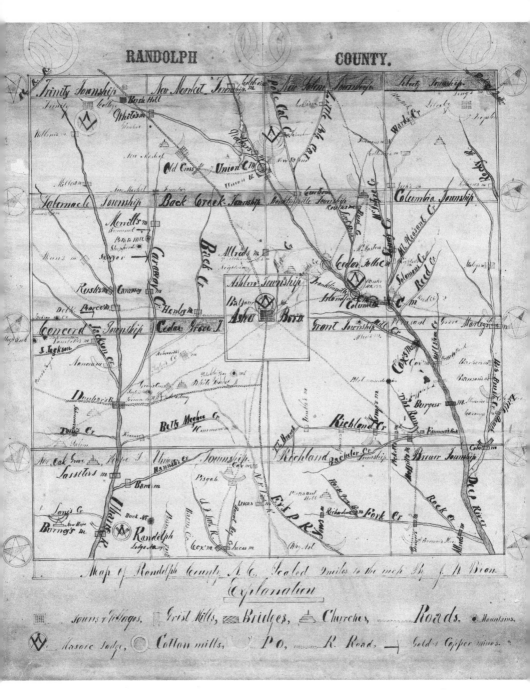

This 1873 map shows cotton mills as well as gold and copper mines. Most cotton mills are located in Franklinville Township, while most mines are found in Tabernacle Township. The map was drawn by J. W. Bean and provided courtesy of the State Archives.

Memorial Hospital in Asheboro was once the home of Capt. Basil J. Fisher. Photograph courtesy of the Randolph County Public Library.

Another potent local industry during and after Reconstruction was converting a portion of the county's sizable corn crop into whiskey. This fostered the two allied industries of pottery and cooperage—potters crafting jugs and other vessels to hold the corn liquor, and coopers creating oak barrels for aging and shipping the brew. Between 1850 and 1900, at least sixteen Seagrove-area coopers produced kegs and barrels for the trade. Both legal and illegal distilleries existed along the creeks and branches of the county, and revenue officers stationed at nearby warehouses collected taxes from those involved in legal business. The whiskey industry thrived until the formation of the Anti-Saloon League in 1890 introduced a period of increased prohibitionist sentiment. Bush Hill (Archdale) served as one of the centers for North Carolina's temperance movement. Supporters organized the state temperance society at Springfield Meeting in 1831. Moses Hammond, a member of Springfield Meeting, presided over the group for a number of years, and in 1888 the Prohibition Party nominated him for lieutenant governor. Eventually, a 1903 state law prohibited the manufacture and sale of spirituous liquors in municipalities of fewer than a thousand residents, thus eliminating the smaller distilleries. Ten years later, Prohibition extended statewide, sounding the death knell for the remaining legal distilleries.

Among the county's early medical practitioners, Dr. William B. Lane of Asheboro achieved notice for a spectacular early medical achievement, as reported in the *Southern Citizen* of October 1, 1839: "Mrs. Curtis, of Sandy Creek in the county, who has been for many years blind from Cataract in the eye, has been happily restored to sight by our skilled physician (and townsman) Dr. William B. Lane. He operated on the right eye some months ago; and she can now see to thread a fine needle and attend to her ordinary business." The article noted that Dr. Lane had recently performed equally successful surgery on Mrs. Curtis's left eye.

The 1860 census listed eighteen physicians residing in Randolph County, plus five "student" physicians, one midwife, and one dentist. Thirty years later the census noted four physicians in Asheboro, six in Randleman, four in Liberty, and seventeen others scattered over other sections of the county. By 1900, physicians practiced in most of the county's larger communities.

During his years of practice, Dr. Jefferson Davis Bulla became the best-known physician in the county. From his home in the Hillsville community, he practiced medicine for seventy-seven years, from 1888 until his death on June 13, 1965, three months shy of his 103rd birthday. Dr. Bulla liked to relate his secret for longevity: "eat a little bit of everything on the table to keep healthy and then push away." After graduating in 1888 from the College of Physicians and Surgeons in Baltimore, he spent a lifetime delivering babies (an estimated five thousand or more) and treating his young patients for minor and serious illnesses and accidents—all from his family residence, still standing in the twenty-first century. Dr. Bulla received a great deal of praise for, among other things, his skill as a fiddle player, for never turning away a patient who could not afford payment, and for his availability twenty-four hours a day.

The period around the turn of the twentieth century brought a proliferation of other, non-medical, services. In 1897 the Bank of Randolph—the only bank between High Point and Rockingham—

opened in Asheboro, with Dr. John Milton Worth as president. The bank formed under the guidance of W. J. Armfield Jr., whose family was active in Guilford County banking. Within a few years, other banks opened in Randleman, Liberty, Ramseur, Coleridge, Seagrove, Franklinville, and Archdale. The county had, for many years, suffered the absence of financial institutions. This resulted in a dearth of circulating currency and a reliance on a bartering system or personal scrip issued by small farmers, merchants, and tradesmen. Citizens had long lamented this situation, including a group assembled in New Salem on July 31, 1837, to petition Congress to establish a national bank. Two individuals raised doubts about its constitutionality, but a large majority passed the motion and sent it to Washington.

Also in the late 1800s, Randolph residents became aware of the need to improve the local transportation network. In order to provide better access to all regions of the county, citizens constructed bridges that would make it possible to safely cross Randolph's numerous creeks, rivers, and streams, where mills were usually sited. The first covered bridges had appeared decades earlier, after county court justices in 1845 authorized the construction of covered bridges at Cedar Falls and Franklinville. Henry Branson Elliott, an owner of the Cedar Falls mill, split the construction costs with the county, each paying $736. This bridge lasted until about 1940, reinforcing the argument that timber bridges that were exposed to the weather decayed within ten to fifteen years, but covered bridges could last a century or more. Builders constructed bridges in the 1880s to get workers, supplies, and finished goods to and from the cotton mills. The largest number of bridges—a total of sixty—were constructed between 1860 and 1920 by private builders who submitted low bids to county commissioners. Known as "kissing bridges," the new structures were favorite travel routes and destinations for young courting couples. Pisgah Covered Bridge, located in the county's southwestern section, 1.5 miles from Pisgah on Little River, is the lone surviving covered bridge in Randolph, a county that probably had more covered bridges than any other in the state. It was built in 1911, with the county paying J. J. Welch forty dollars for the forty-foot span.

The Pisgah Covered Bridge, built in 1911 at a cost of forty dollars, was one of only two covered bridges still standing in North Carolina in the twenty-first century. Located in Union Township on a shallow branch of the Little River, it was destroyed by heavy rainfall in August of 2003 but has since been rebuilt. Photograph by the author.

Ushering in an era of dramatic change, the first passenger and freight train arrived in Asheboro in July 1889. The community held a celebration on July 4 commemorating the arrival of the High Point, Randleman, Asheboro, and Southern Railroad (HPRA & Southern). The fanfare attracted hundreds of people from a wide area, many of them camping out for days to witness the arrival of the first iron horse. Prior to this time, Fayetteville, North Carolina, and Cheraw, South Carolina, had been the primary trade outlets for Randolph farmers and industries. The new rail service, via High Point, allowed markets to expand.

By 1894, upon completion of the Asheboro and Montgomery Railroad (A&M) from the town of Star to Asheboro, about seventy-six miles of rail had been laid in the county. In 1897 the A&M merged with the Aberdeen and West End to form the Aberdeen and Asheboro Railroad (A&A). (The Page family owned both companies; in 1912 the family sold the A&A Railroad to Norfolk and Southern.) The two existing railroad companies—the HPRA & Southern and the A&A—constructed rail depots in Asheboro, each competing for an assortment of freight ranging from finished lumber and crossties to barrels of flour. Between 1900 and 1935, when the HPRA & Southern discontinued passenger service, the A&A served Asheboro with five daily trains. The last A&A passenger train departed on July 7, 1945, and a few years later freight service fell to one train per day. Since that time, Liberty has been the only stop on Southern Railway's main line.

The arrival of the railroads brought changes to Asheboro's business district, from the area around the old courthouse square to present-day Sunset Avenue, the site of the first train depot. Lt. Col. Alexander Cary McAlister's family members established Asheboro's first hosiery mill around the close of the nineteenth century. At about that same time Asheboro Furniture Company and Asheboro Chair Company commenced operations. Branson's 1894 directory listed the following Randolph County enterprises, practitioners, and institutions: 50 gold mines, 12 textile mills, 1 hosiery mill, 1 broom works, 2 shoe manufacturers, 5 tanneries and harness factories, 2 lumber manufacturing companies, 1 carriage-buggy works, 2 chair factories, 3 brick and tile works, 9 potteries, 7 wood and milling companies, 1 stove factory, 2 shuttle block factories, 1 sash/blind factory, 1 cigar factory, 8 lawyers, 4 hotels, 12 boarding houses, 7 roller mills, 85 gristmills, 30 sawmills, 45 ministers, 2 weekly and monthly newspapers, 35 physicians, 81 post offices, 8 academies, and 136 public schools.

By 1900, Randolph County had experienced significant growth, and its county seat of Asheboro could finally boast of offering more than merely a courthouse and a small trading area for farmers. Accordingly, builders completed a new courthouse in 1909, erected in the cornfield purchased from Col. Alexander C. McAlister. Development steadily continued into the early twentieth century: the Moffitt family opened Asheboro Wood and Iron Works, W. D. Stedman started Stedman Bobbin Factory, Capt. A. E. Burns established a casket factory, and E. H. Cranford created Asheboro Veneer Company.

CHAPTER FIVE

Randolph from 1900 to 1945

*T*hose residing in Randolph County at the beginning of the twentieth century had experienced a period of great change. From older men and women who had lived through the era since the Civil War and Reconstruction, to younger people who witnessed the further growth of towns and commerce, all had encountered numerous societal changes. The county's population (28,232 in 1900) had quadrupled during the 1800s, cotton mills hummed, additional industries developed, and a bank had finally been established. In the early decades of the twentieth century, construction of such infrastructure as electric plants, telephone lines, and all-weather roads increased at a steady pace.

Electricity and telephone service emerged and expanded early in the 1900s. Electricity arrived in Asheboro in 1905 when the town contracted with a private company to build a power-generating system and transmission lines, which the municipality took over in 1911. Thirteen years later the town granted a franchise to Carolina Power and Light Company (CP&L). W. H. Watkins built a power plant for Ramseur's cotton mill in 1911; he also sold power to private customers until 1924 when the town built a plant on Deep River, then promptly sold it to CP&L. Nearby Liberty obtained its power in 1916 from Liberty Chair Company, which had installed a gasoline-powered electric generator that the town soon purchased; the franchise was later sold to CP&L as well. A limited number of Randleman customers received their electricity, beginning in 1909, from Randolph Power Company, until Duke Power extended lines to Archdale and Randleman in 1927. In contrast to the townspeople, many rural residents had to depend on gasoline-powered generators or live without electricity until 1939, when Randolph Electric Membership was franchised and began providing electricity to rural areas. In 1900, even before the county enjoyed electricity, it boasted two telephone companies: Asheboro Telephone, organized three years prior by a group of local citizens, and Randleman Telephone.

Swan[n]anoa Street, in downtown Liberty, as it appeared in the early twentieth century. Note the telephone poles. Photograph courtesy of the State Archives.

Other towns soon had local phone service, but not until 1954 did the Randolph Telephone Membership Corporation begin serving rural areas in Randolph and adjacent counties.

A 1907 state law provided funds to assist Randolph County in establishing high schools in three predominantly rural areas: Farmer, Liberty, and Trinity. In an effort to combat illiteracy, the General Assembly in 1913 levied a state property tax of five cents valuation to aid in extending the school year to six months. The legislature also passed a compulsory attendance law for children aged eight to twelve; additionally, the law addressed child labor, prohibiting the employment of children under twelve. Statistics from the Randolph Board of Education showed that, in 1915, Randolph had a white population of 18,850 over the age of ten, of whom 2,188 (11.6 percent) were illiterate. County superintendent T. Fletcher Bulla's report of January 14, 1914, showed a total of 105 schools for white students and twenty-two for black students, with a breakdown of white and black school districts and apportionment of county funds on the basis of student population and need. World War I hindered some of the school programs because of the loss of male teachers and principals to the military. Less-qualified and less-experienced teachers, mainly female, replaced the male educators. However, after the war, the General Assembly provided special building funds for loans to counties, resulting in better-equipped educational facilities, plus new buildings in eight local school districts. In 1926 Randolph County Training School (later renamed Central High School), for African American students in Asheboro, moved into a new brick building financed with local and state funds and assistance from the Julius Rosenwald Foundation. This additional funding provided better educational opportunities for African American students.

The fifteen-year period prior to World War I saw a notable increase in industrial growth within the county. Hosiery manufacturing and allied fields expanded, providing employment for large numbers of people, and continued to do so for a half century. The establishment of the county's first hosiery mill by L. A. Spencer, A. N. Bulla, and S. G. Newlin in Randleman in 1893 prefaced this twentieth-century industrial expansion. Many authorities have regarded the Randleman Hosiery Mill as a pioneer in the Piedmont's hosiery industry. The mill annually produced approximately 360,000 pairs of ribbed cotton stockings for women and children. The company soon opened a plant in High Point. With the 1909 purchase by D. B. McCrary and his brother-in-law, T. H. Redding, of the small, two-year-old, near-bankrupt Acme Hosiery Mills in Asheboro, the Randolph County and High Point area began its ascent to arguably become the hosiery capital of North Carolina, if not the nation.

Chisholm C. Cranford's determination, acumen, and farsighted business approach would make him one of the county's foremost businessmen. Twenty years old, he arrived in Asheboro in 1895, moving from Concord Township, located west of the county seat. Before he entered the furniture business and after taking menial jobs to prove himself, Cranford's early enterprises consisted of the Asheboro Roller Mills and Southern Crown Milling Company. In 1908 he purchased the Randolph Chair Company from G. G. Hendricks and operated it until converting the building into a hosiery mill. With partners he organized three chair and furniture companies and a veneer company.

An early-twentieth-century photograph of millworkers in front of an Acme-McCrary Corporation mill. The company was established in 1909 and is still in business. Photograph courtesy of the Randolph County Public Library.

Equally enterprising was the Ross family. In 1904, it purchased Asheboro Lumber and Manufacturing from C. C. McAlister and formed a company they named Home Building Materials, with J. D. Ross as president and Arthur Ross as secretary-treasurer. L. Ferree Ross later bought out the other family members, and his sister Esther Ross soon joined him as secretary. The company also operated the Asheboro Coffin and Casket Company. In its prime, Home Building Materials was one of the county's largest employers. The 1920 business index listed a work force of seven in the casket plant and one hundred in the home-building products division.

In 1911 Randleman Manufacturing Company, Naomi Falls Manufacturing Company, Plaidville Mills, and Marie Antoinette Mills were acquired by Deep River Mills, with J. C. Watkins as president, T. A. Hunter as secretary, and R. P. Deal as manager. Deep River Mills became Randleman's largest employer, with some six hundred workers, two dams, and four plants located on three hundred acres of land. Another local venture, the Randleman Chair Company, organized by John R. Ferree (son of John H. Ferree), opened about 1905 and operated until around 1915.

Hundreds of men from Randolph County served in World War I. Company K, 120th Infantry, of the Thirtieth "Old Hickory" Division, was one group of local doughboys still remembered for their heroic actions in the trenches of the Hindenburg line in France. Company K consisted primarily of men from Asheboro and other parts of Randolph County. The company served in Texas in 1916 during the Mexican border campaign, returning to Asheboro in March 1917 from El Paso. Immediately after the United States' declaration of war on Germany in April, the men mobilized. On September 2 the unit joined the Thirtieth Division at Camp Sevier, South Carolina, for reorganization and training. The division then deployed to Callis, France, arriving May 24, 1918.

The Old Hickory Division saw action on the western front at Ypres, the Hindenburg line, the Battle of Bellicourt, the Battle of Montbrehain, and the Battle of La Selle River. After further training, the Thirtieth Division, along with the Twenty-seventh Division of New York, was assigned a position alongside the British army in northern France, near the Belgian border. This segment of the British army occupied a position opposite the famed Hindenburg line. The well-placed German line occupied a defensive position well adapted for machine-gun defense. For months the Germans had developed every feature of the area, making it an almost invulnerable front, with trenches, barbed wire, and other sharp objects enabling easy troop movement within. The Allies mounted an extensive attack on September 29, 1918, at 5:50 A.M. The Allied field artillery were ordered to lay down fixed barrages for four minutes at a time, cease for four-minute stretches to allow the infantry forces to advance one hundred yards, then resume firing. The weather cooperated—mist, low clouds, and poor visibility provided good cover for the advancing troops. Lt. Clarence J. Lovett of Asheboro, the battalion scout officer, had gone out the night before with engineers to mark the starting line with tape. The group endured German machine-gun fire throughout the process.

Capt. Ben F. Dixon Jr. of Gastonia, North Carolina, was a graduate of Trinity College and Columbia University. In 1898, during the Spanish-American War, the seventeen-year-old Ben and his twin brother, Wright, enlisted in the U.S. Army. They engaged in active duty in Cuba. During World War I, Wright, by then a

Many men from Randolph County served in World War I. In the photograph above, the soldiers of Company K dig trenches at Camp Sevier, South Carolina, about 1917. Photograph courtesy of the Randolph County Public Library.

lieutenant, served in a machine-gun company of the 120th Infantry. In a letter to an older brother, Wright wrote an account of the attack on the Hindenburg line as related to him by one of his twin brother's sergeants. The sergeant noted that "Captain [Ben Dixon] was the coolest man I have ever seen." The following is an account of Ben's actions as related by the sergeant:

After the barrage came, Captain Dixon ordered the men forward to follow him. He had progressed about three hundred yards when he took a machine-gun bullet through his right leg, just below the knee. The sergeant offered to take him back to the relative safety of the starting point, but Captain Dixon refused. The two caught up with the others, the captain limping along. A few minutes later, Ben Dixon took another bullet, this time through his left upper arm and into his back. Again he refused to turn back. Then Dixon started off at a half-trot, holding his hand over his arm, all the while telling his men to slow their pace. In his final admonition he yelled "remember, keep your heads, and reach your objectives."

Captain Dixon, who had planned to set up a law practice in Asheboro after the war, suffered mortal wounds about halfway to his goal. His men buried him on a knoll overlooking the Hindenburg line.

All officers and senior noncommissioned officers in the assault were either killed or wounded, and it fell upon platoon sergeant Colon Bunting to lead Company K. The first sergeant to lead, Ernest E. Bunting (Colon's brother), suffered a serious throat wound in the attack and temporarily lost his voice. Top sergeant Thomas J. McDowell, while leading his men, suffered mortal wounds soon after Captain Dixon succumbed. Cpl. Jake Brown also died during the attack, as did Sgt. William O. Forrester of Ramseur, Sgt. Hal E. Richardson of Star, and Pvt. John Kivett of Asheboro. A Lieutenant Lovett reported that the troops reached their objective about eleven in the morning, captured the mouth of the San Quentin Canal in their advance, and passed through the Hindenburg line. At the mouth of the canal they fired bullets and grenades at German

machine-gun nests and took 115 prisoners. However, of the nearly two hundred men of Company K who started the attack, only twenty-six reached the objective. The remainder were either killed or wounded over the three-thousand-yard expanse of the advance line.

Capt. Ben F. Dixon, Company K, 120th Infantry, 30th Division, American Expeditionary Forces, World War I. KIA in France. Photograph courtesy of the Randolph County Public Library.

The remnants of Company K returned home in April 1919 and quietly resumed civilian life. On Armistice Day 1925, members of Company K and other county veterans assembled at Old Hickory Café in downtown Asheboro to organize a post of the American Legion, later named Dixon Post 45.

Many Randolphians served in other units in France during World War I. At least four were stationed with a former Randleman physician, Dr. John Wesley Long of Greensboro, at Base Hospital No. 65—a new hospital at Kerhouon (near Brest), France. They arrived just before the Meuse offensive of September 1918. The hospital lacked barracks or running water. During October 1918, an average of sixty-six deaths occurred every twenty-four hours at this hospital, as the Spanish influenza pandemic raged. In November the institution suffered only twenty-eight deaths. The unit began with twenty-eight hundred beds and became one of the largest field hospitals in France, eventually containing forty-two hundred beds. Soon after the enlargement of the hospital, the armistice came, and the wounded, the sick, and the exhausted soldiers were eager to return home.

Back home, the same influenza was also widespread, with many families forced to remain indoors, unable to function normally. Neighbors well enough to do so prepared food for the ill and left it outside doorways, afraid to come into contact with the contagious. Randolph County suffered 105 flu-related deaths. Especially severe for three months, beginning in October 1918, the epidemic continued throughout the winter of 1918–1919.

Voluntary rationing of numerous items lasted throughout the war, with some days designated "wheatless, sweetless, and heatless." The patriotism of civilians sparked the sales of liberty stamps and bonds, even among schoolchildren. The junior and senior Red Cross chapters rolled bandages and knitted sweaters for the military hospitals.

The return of servicemen from all military branches in the months following the November 1918 armistice was a joyous occasion for many families. For others who had lost loved ones, it was a time of sorrow. But Randolphians looked forward to better times and continuing growth and progress.

Not until 1915 did the county's first graded and paved road appear—a fifteen-mile stretch from Asheboro to the southern border—ushering in the era of the automobile, five years after the first motor cars arrived locally. Asheboro got its first paved street in 1920. In 1921 the North Carolina General Assembly approved a fifty-million-dollar bond issue for statewide road construction. Within seven years a network of roads connected all county seats.

The General Assembly did not, however, provide funding for public libraries until 1940. Before the emergence of public and private schools in Randolph, a number of churches, especially Friends meetings, assembled book collections to lend to people in the community. These served as forerunners of the public libraries, the first of which appeared between 1819 and 1828. During those years, three libraries opened in the New Salem, Caraway, and Ebenezer communities—among the first thirty-two libraries in the state. In the 1930s the Asheboro Woman's Club, with encouragement and financial assistance from Elvira Worth Jackson, began planning to establish public libraries under the umbrella of the Randolph Public Library system. Already open was the Franklinville library, established in 1924 by John W. Clark, primary owner of the cotton and flour mills there. The Great Depression delayed the construction of other libraries. The Asheboro Woman's Club organized the Asheboro Public Library in 1936, followed by public libraries in Ramseur, Liberty, Randleman, and East Asheboro. In its first decade the library system's holdings expanded from one thousand to fifty-five thousand volumes.

Alongside the growing public library system, civic clubs and organizations catering to people of similar interests emerged in the years between the two world wars. In Asheboro a group of women organized the Friday Afternoon Book Club. David S. Coltrane was appointed as the first Randolph County farm agent in 1917. The year 1926 brought the establishment of the Asheboro Rotary Club, followed in two years by the Asheboro Kiwanis Club, the Liberty Rotary Club, and the county's first Girl Scout troops. In 1936 the Sorosis Club formed in Asheboro, and an early project sponsored school concerts by the North Carolina Symphony. Two years later, Randleman and Ramseur residents organized Lions Clubs. The county appointed Laura Brashears its first home economist in 1939.

The post-World War I years also brought a revival of the local pottery trade. Only a few potters were still at their homemade kick wheels in the Seagrove area when, in 1915, visitor Juliana Busbee found and purchased a pie dish that she immediately recognized as a type of pottery her husband Jacques had been searching for to sell in his small New York shop. Jacques was dissatisfied with the wares he had been obtaining from art potters in Pinehurst, created, he claimed, for the Yankee tourist trade. The Busbees traced the pie dish to the studio of a potter named Ben Owen. Jacques Busbee subsequently partnered with Owen, an eighteen-year-old who had learned the trade from his father. By 1917 Busbee had purchased land just over the Randolph line in Moore County and named it Jugtown, thereby reviving the pottery tradition in portions of Randolph, Moore, Montgomery, and Lee counties. Gradually, other potters dusted off their potter's wheels and began throwing pots, and newcomers attracted to the area built upon the pottery tradition. The craft rose like the phoenix from the memories of the Chriscoe, Cole, Craven, Luck, McNeill, and Owen families, who had lived within a five-mile radius of one another in the Seagrove area since their ancestors had immigrated there from Staffordshire, England, in the eighteenth century.

The North Carolina Museum of History holds several pieces of Ben W. Owen's pottery in its collection, including this Persian jar in Chinese blue glaze with four strap handles and rope banding. Owen made it sometime between 1923 and 1947. Photograph courtesy of the North Carolina Museum of History.

The New York dealer and the teenage potter seemed destined for success. Jacques Busbee, an artist and Raleigh native, was interested in the artistic appeal of pottery, as well as the traditional utilitarian wares of crocks, jugs, churns, bowls, and dishes. The young Owen had begun training as a potter by digging clay from nearby bogs and fields, mixing, blending, and working the material into the proper color and texture. His skill and eagerness to learn led to Jugtown's thirty-five years of prosperity. Owen attained the status of master potter, a title of distinction and recognition accorded him by his peers and the public. His highly regarded work, influenced by the Oriental masters, was exhibited in top galleries, including the Smithsonian Institution and the Metropolitan Museum of Art. Owen continued to employ the original techniques he had learned for firing his salt-glazed and orange earthenware pottery in big groundhog (earthen) wood-burning kilns behind his log workshop. He apparently never lost his fascination with the way heat altered the chunks of clay he shaped, admitting he never ceased to feel amazed and thrilled when the kilns were opened. Thus began a pottery revival that took another half century to attract attention outside the immediate area.

In the late 1910s, particularly after the war, numerous new hosiery mills sprang up in Randolph County. In 1917, Chisholm C. Cranford established Asheboro Hosiery Mills to manufacture men's half-hosiery (socks), and later entered the ladies' field. Staley Hosiery Mills opened the next year. In 1924 McCrary Hosiery Mills commenced operations, targeting the female market, working along with its previously established Acme Hosiery Mills. T. A. Johnson and E. W. Fuller established Dependable Hosiery in Liberty in 1927. One year later two brothers, Charles G. and Joseph C. Bossong, organized Bossong Hosiery Mills in Asheboro to produce women's hose. During the depression years, in 1932, Arthur Ross established Tip-Top Hosiery Mills to manufacture items for men.

Randolph's chair-making industry also broadened during and after the First World War. In 1914 Chisholm C. Cranford formed National Chair Company, later acquired by W. Clyde Lucas. Gregson Manufacturing, established in 1921, began creating cane-bottomed chairs in Liberty, later expanding to become a major manufacturer of school and institutional seating. The Carolina Rocker—the chair design that gained worldwide fame and the moniker "Kennedy Rocker" when a physician prescribed it for President John F. Kennedy's back condition—dates its beginnings to 1926, when William Carl Page and Arthur Presnell started P&P Chair Company in Asheboro.

President John F. Kennedy favored the chair that P&P sold as the "Carolina Rocker" because it helped relieve his chronic back pain. Photograph by Robert Knudsen, White House, and courtesy of the John F. Kennedy Presidential Library and Museum, Boston.

Another area of growth during and after World War I was the increased availability of medical services. Dr. Charles E. Wilkerson and his wife, Lula Phillips Wilkerson, a nurse, opened Ferree Memorial Hospital in Randleman in 1911 at the former residence of John H. Ferree. The hospital also offered nurses' training but closed in 1915, the same year that Dr. J. F. Miller, his wife, and several other nurses opened Miller Hospital in Asheboro. This facility closed when Dr. Miller entered the army in 1918; Mrs. Miller died that same year, a victim of the influenza pandemic. In 1919 physicians C. A. and Ray W. Hayworth established Memorial Hospital in Asheboro. When Dr. Ray Hayworth left for navy duty (he later became the chief medical officer on a hospital ship during World War II), Dr. George H. Sumner and Dr. W. L. Lambert joined the hospital staff, and the facility expanded to house fifty beds. The hospital closed in 1931 because of Dr. C. A. Hayworth's health problems, and the building (the Fisher estate's original manor house) burned soon afterward. In 1919 Dr. Wilkerson and his wife returned

Asheboro's P&P Chair Company, created in 1926 by William Carl Page and Arthur Presnell, later manufactured the famous "Kennedy Rocker." Photograph courtesy of the State Archives.

to the county from southern Sudan, where they had served as medical missionaries for the Presbyterian Mission Board. The couple purchased a house near Sophia and set up a fifteen-bed hospital after installing an electric generator and a plumbing system. They moved to Greensboro in 1926 after closing the hospital; however, they opened a satellite medical office in Randleman.

As the century progressed, other medical institutions emerged. In 1925 the Randolph County Health Department was established in Asheboro, with Dr. George H. Sumner installed as medical officer. Two years earlier Lillie Pearl Wood had become the county's first female lab technician. Randolph Hospital opened in 1932 as a private corporation, built with community and corporate donations, and matching funds from the Duke Endowment. D. B. McCrary served as trustees chairman (1931–1946), succeeded by his son, Charles Walker McCrary Sr., who held the position until his death. Dr. George W. Joyner, the first resident physician and chief surgeon, practiced medicine at the hospital until his 1978 retirement.

Barnes-Griffin Clinic operated as a thirty-six-bed clinic in downtown Asheboro from 1938 to 1962, specializing in maternity care and birthing. The original physicians were Dr. Dempsey Barnes and Dr. Harvey Lee Griffin.

As in previous generations, new leaders appeared in the early twentieth century, Asheboro's William Cicero Hammer prominent among them. Hammer represented the thirteen counties of the old Seventh District in the U.S. Congress for five terms, from 1920 until his death in office on September 26, 1930. His career of service to the people included stints as educator, mayor, public defender, newspaper editor, and state legislator. Although Hammer was credited as editor of the *Asheboro Courier* newspaper, his wife, Minnie Hancock Hammer, actually directed the operation in his absence during his terms as district solicitor and then congressman. In 1924, to combat the Democrat leanings of the *Courier,* A. I. Ferree and Wiley Ward established the *Randolph Tribune* as a Republican voice. Roy Cox Sr. purchased the *Tribune* in 1934, combined the two newspapers four years later, and began publishing two editions a week as the *Courier-Tribune.* Chatham News Publishing Company's *Liberty News* first appeared in 1939.

When servicemen returned from World War I, they anticipated not only a warm welcome home but also prosperity, well-paying jobs, and settling into rewarding lives with family and friends. But after a brief flourish in business and building activities, along came the Great Depression of the 1930s. Many Randolph County citizens (especially those involved in agriculture, who could at least provide their own food or items for barter) endured the Great Depression better than the nation as a whole, where the unemployment rate was around 25 percent during the years 1930 to 1939. Hardest hit locally was Randleman, where the cotton mills closed and the city was without a payroll from 1930 until 1934. Other afflicted plants survived by cutting wages and shortening the workweek.

Because prices remained at very low levels, individuals with sufficient cash holdings enjoyed an advantage. However, others lost their businesses, homes, or automobiles because of an inability to maintain payments. Locally, the first five years of the 1930s were the toughest for many to endure. President Roosevelt and Congress initiated relief programs that they hoped would kick-start the national economy, but the Great Depression crippled the country until the United States entered World War II. Congress introduced a number of federal programs, including the Public Works Administration (PWA) and the Works Progress Administration (WPA)—both of which sponsored building and infrastructure projects—and the Civilian Conservation Corps, which established a camp near Ramseur for young men unable to find work. The workers participated in such soil conservation and forestry activities as building farm ponds, planting pine seedlings, clearing out brush, and terracing land.

A new Asheboro post office and municipal building were fruits of those working on the WPA projects. The nine-hole Asheboro Municipal Golf Course (1935), the first golf course in the county, was another. Laura Worth, employed with federal funds as the first county historian, helped inventory and catalog records contained in the Randolph County Courthouse. These records were voluminous because Randolph was among those North Carolina counties whose records were not at some point destroyed by fire. These federally funded projects ceased with the advent of World War II.

Laura Stimson Worth was Randolph's first county historian from 1934 to 1974. Photograph courtesy of the Randolph County Public Library.

During World War II, a total of 14,328 men registered for the draft at the two county draft boards, and more than forty-four hundred Randolph County citizens, including women and African Americans, went on to serve in the armed forces. The home front was united as the civilian population worked long hours producing goods deemed essential for the war effort while "making do" with meager supplies and the rationing of food, tires, and fuel for homes and vehicles. The official War Department casualty records indicate that fifty-six Randolph men died in combat during World War II;

eight other soldiers later succumbed to mortal wounds, and twenty-two died from causes unrelated to combat. Records of the War and Navy Departments show that a total of 101 Randolph men died; however, the figure increases to 135 if one includes men who volunteered at recruiting stations outside the county, or men who were drafted while working elsewhere. Those who died in service were honored by having their names painted on a Gold Star Memorial Board, sponsored by the Asheboro Rotary Club, at the courthouse. This memorial was updated as needed throughout the war.

Among those who gave their lives was Capt. Walter A. Bunch III, whose father had served as mayor of Asheboro for a decade and had stepped down in May, just before his son was killed in action in France on July 9, 1944.

TSgt. Benjamin F. Lambeth, 22, son of Mr. and Mrs. T. J. Lambeth of Asheboro, exemplified great courage and received decorations for his many feats. He earned a combat commission as second lieutenant in March 1945 with the army's Fifth Front in Italy for "exemplary service throughout the Italian Campaign." He also received the Silver Star for combat gallantry. The citation stated that Lambeth killed twenty-five Germans, wounded seven others, and routed the remainder of a patrol. He also received a Purple Heart and two battle stars during his service as a platoon leader in a rifle company.

Floyd Harrison Trogdon, son of William H. and Ethel Hendrix Trogdon of Asheboro, was the second man from Randolph to achieve the rank of brigadier general. He entered World War II as an aviation cadet and retired after thirty years of distinguished service, which included the Korean and Vietnam Wars. In World War II, he served as a B-24 navigator and completed fifty combat missions over Germany, France, Italy, and elsewhere in southern Europe. Trogdon was credited with the destruction of an ME 109 aircraft.

During the war, local industries, especially those producing textile goods, experienced federally imposed production quotas. Plants struggled to comply with these quotas, primarily because of manpower shortages resulting from the large numbers of men and women in military service. Furthermore, many individuals had left the county to work in shipyards and aircraft factories.

Local businesses recruited workers from nearby counties, a task made more difficult because of gasoline rationing. Car pools and retired and recast school buses were utilized to the fullest.

Although the Great Depression had a significant negative impact on Randolph County industries, Stedman Manufacturing Company survived, restarting production lines after closing for several months because of competition from cheap handkerchiefs imported from Japan. Sulon B. Stedman had founded the company in 1930 to make handkerchiefs, and during World War II the company produced tee shirts for the U.S. Navy. In 1945 Stedman shifted production almost entirely to men's tee shirts in order to meet the navy's demands. After the war the company designed boys' and men's underwear and sportswear lines and ceased the production of handkerchiefs.

Even the county's hosiery mills operated in a military mode as they produced stockings for the women in uniform and socks for the men. However, with silk supplies from Japan and China cut off by import restrictions, women's hosiery was fashioned with rayon and cotton yarns. McCrary Industry's Sapona Mill processed nylon yarn for parachutes, ponchos, and other military applications, and the government issued a certificate of necessity (a priority permit to purchase building materials and provide labor for projects deemed vital to the war effort) to build a large addition to the plant. Many years after the end of the war, a news service article from Washington revealed that the U.S. government's strategic plan listed Randolph County as a "quite probable target" for enemy air attacks because of the county's efforts in supplying vital war needs, especially stockings, which authorities deemed a necessity for the morale of servicewomen.

During the war, victory gardens were common among town dwellers and those in Randolph's rural areas. Items such as coffee, tea, sugar, meat, and even shoes were rationed with coupon books, and people saved sugar and gasoline coupons for special cakes and family gatherings. Virtually every family responded to the call to buy war bonds and war stamps to provide additional funds. Because of the close proximity of Fort Bragg and Camp Mackall and the frequent military maneuvers in the area, Randolph residents often encountered convoys of soldiers, who eagerly accepted invitations for home-cooked meals. The local American Red Cross chapter

HOW TO USE YOUR GASOLINE RATION BOOK

This book has six pages of eight coupons each. Each coupon is numbered and is good only as follows: Coupons numbered 1, during first and second months. Coupons numbered 2, during third and fourth months. Coupons numbered 3, during fifth and sixth months. Coupons numbered 4, during seventh and eighth months. Coupons numbered 5, during ninth and tenth months. Coupons numbered 6, during eleventh and twelfth months.

Each coupon is good for ONE "A" UNIT of gasoline. The number of gallons which each coupon gives you the right to buy will depend upon the demands of the war program; therefore, the value of the unit may be changed. Any change in value will be publicly announced by the Office of Price Administration.

Do not loosen or tear coupons from the book. Detached coupons must not be honored by the dealer. When buying gasoline, hand the book to the service station attendant. Only he is allowed to remove coupons. He must remove enough coupons to cover the number of gallons of gasoline purchased. If your purchase is only a part of a unit, the attendant must nevertheless remove an entire coupon.

The station attendant is permitted to deliver gasoline only into the tank of the vehicle described on the front cover of this book. Do not ask him to violate the law.

A gasoline ration book from World War II. Photograph courtesy of the Randolph County Public Library.

recruited women to knit sweaters and roll bandages, as they did during World War I.

For Randolph County, the first half of the twentieth century consisted of periods of progress and stagnation. At times, industries flourished, and improvements in infrastructure accompanied other signs of social and economic advancement. The Great Depression and the resulting deprivation and widespread unemployment, followed by World War II, brought a temporary halt to this prosperity. However, with the war over, the second half of the century in Randolph County would be a time of rapid growth in virtually all sectors of the economy. Family life and other aspects of people's lives would change greatly as well.

CHAPTER SIX

Ushering in a New Millennium

For Randolph County, one can categorize the years following World War II as a time of diversification, both economically and socially. County leaders and businessmen lured international companies to Randolph to build industrial plants, which introduced new products into an economy previously dominated by such homegrown industries as hosiery and wood products. The efforts not only stimulated a significant population increase but also served as a catalyst for the development of Randolph Technical Institute (now Randolph Community College) and its sprawling campus. The institute offered general education courses and two-year college transfer programs; short courses enabled men and women to obtain the knowledge and skills required by high-tech industries.

The visionary Chisholm C. Cranford, already a competitor in the county's hosiery and furniture industries, keenly promoted diversification by erecting two large buildings in 1947 to attract new enterprises. That year he helped convince Union Carbide Corporation to establish a local plant for producing Eveready (later called Energizer) batteries. Nurtured by a boom in the postwar economy, the plant quickly grew large enough to generate most of the D-cell batteries sold in the country. Union Carbide expanded its original plant threefold within a decade, making it the largest flashlight battery plant in the United States. It soon built a second plant in north Asheboro to produce other battery sizes, alkaline and specialty batteries, and department store brands.

Also in 1947, Cranford helped convince William Klopman to locate a Klopman Mills plant in North Asheboro for weaving blended cotton–synthetic greige (unfinished) goods. Klopman later expanded the Asheboro plant and located, at the site, the corporate offices and transportation center for ten Klopman plants and seven thousand employees. Within seven years, after taking over plants at Central Falls, Klopman Mills was Randolph County's largest employer, with twenty-five hundred employees and an annual payroll of $11.5 million. The company merged all of its operations into the previously established Burlington Industries in 1957.

A company founded before the war, Stedman Manufacturing branched out in the 1950s to fabricate a full line of men's and boys' underwear. Sportswear became the largest part of the business, with five manufacturing divisions and thirteen plants producing underwear, knit fabrics, and elastic. It became the second-largest privately owned company in the United States producing knit sportswear for boys and men. After the death of Sulon B. Stedman, his son W. David Stedman became president and chief executive. David sold the company in 1986 to Hanes Underwear.

In the postwar years a number of outside companies relocated to Randolph County. Among these was the General Electric Company, which established a plant in Asheboro in 1952 to make heating pads and electric blankets, and later expanded to manufacture a variety of small household appliances. By 1976 the annual payroll had grown to $7.5 million, and more than a hundred employees had been with the company since the local plant opened. An industry new to Randolph, United Brass Works, relocated to Randleman from Brooklyn, New York, in 1958, occupying a building vacated by Burlington Mills, which had closed its hosiery plant. The firm manufactured pressure valves for boilers and sprinkler systems.

After World War II, longtime citizens of Randolph grasped opportunities to initiate new ventures, including the production of shoes, wearing apparel, canned foods, country hams, and an assortment of other goods. Bartlette Burkhead Walker entered the shoe business by selling surplus GI shoes to rural stores. In 1956 he decided to manufacture his own, beginning with work shoes and broadening to cowboy boots and men's dress shoes. By the early 1960s, B. B. Walker Company's sales force included fifty full-time salesmen with accounts in all fifty states and Puerto Rico. Some seven hundred employees in a manufacturing space of 225,000 square feet produced two million shoes annually. In the early 1960s Walker and Albert A. Harrelson Jr. formed Harrelson Rubber Company, a wholly owned subsidiary of the Walker Company, to manufacture its Harrelson brand of retread rubber for motor vehicle tires. Oliver Rubber, the parent company of Cooper Tire and Rubber, later acquired this division.

In the textile industry, an established New York manufacturer appeared on the Randolph scene when it acquired an area company. I. Schneierson and Sons of New York purchased Randleman's Randolph Underwear Company in 1944, and the operation continued to manufacture lingerie. The company became known as A. J. Schneierson, and by the early 1950s its 350 employees produced some 60,000 items per week.

Also entering the textile trade were several other companies. John F. Redding and A. D. Potter opened Pinehurst Textiles in 1946 to make lingerie. In 1956 Potter sold his interest to D. Clyde Graves and established Potter Manufacturing Company, producing lingerie in partnership with his brother, A. J. Potter. Blue Gem Manufacturing, a maker of ladies' sportswear, pants, skirts, and shirts, opened a branch in Asheboro in 1948 and sold the plant to Blue Bell in 1971. In 1953 Hugh Callicutt formed a partnership with Larry Millburg to manufacture lingerie in Asheboro. Their operation quickly reached a daily production level of about 12,000 pieces of underwear. Mr. Jeans, a company new to the area, came to Randleman in 1965 and began producing sportswear, combining three years later with U.S. Industries. A number of necktie plants also appeared in the county, including Bost Neckwear, Tie-Rite, and Salem Neckwear.

Further growth occurred in the food industry, notably in processing. Mountain View Canning Company was started in 1947 by Alfred Spencer and Ivey B. Luck to provide home canning of local products (vegetables and meats) for people in the Seagrove area. Clay Presnell joined the company in 1948. When C. C. Smith bought an interest five years later, the owners changed the company name to Luck's Incorporated and expanded in order to produce a greater range of items. Luck's later merged with American Home Products, immediately increasing the production lines to accommodate twenty-four meat and vegetable items.

Various manufacturers of meat products began business during this time. Carl Hamlet organized Randolph Packing Company in 1947 to process beef. Soon thereafter, Millikan Sausage entered the field to process sausage and other pork products. Hancock's Old Fashion Country Ham was founded by Wilbert Hancock of Franklinville in 1955 to cure, slice, and vacuum-pack country hams, growing into one of the largest companies of this type in the country. Hancock sold to the Lance Company in 1974, and Gwaltney of Smithfield

Ivey B. Luck, co-founder of the company that eventually became Luck's Inc., stands next to an oversized replica of canned beans, which is presumably a promotional tool. Photograph courtesy of the Randolph County Public Library.

later acquired the operation in order to generate a new line of smoked-pork products. A number of other country ham companies operated in the county: Cloverleaf, Phillips Brothers, Thomas Brothers, and Yates Country Hams. These operations were much smaller than Hancock, with sales mainly in Randolph County and vicinity.

Additional food-related businesses appeared and flourished. In 1948 Russell Walker, his brother Al, and Clarence Davis, opened the first Food Line supermarkets in Asheboro. Previously existing competitors included Big Bear, A&P, Colonial, and smaller local grocers. Over the next two decades Food Line grew into a chain of thirteen stores in five counties before its 1978 acquisition by Lowe's Foods.

The local hosiery industry continued to thrive. A resumption in the production of nylon yarn at the end of World War II prompted established mills to add new employees and high-speed machines and to enter the seamless hosiery field. Sapona Manufacturing Company in Cedar Falls processed nylon for hosiery and sold its yarn to competitors and its parent company, Acme-McCrary Hosiery. Among the larger enterprises were Laughlin Hosiery Mill (incorporated in 1938), Richard Grey Hosiery, Vuncannon Hosiery, Charmeuse, and Banner Hosiery in Asheboro. At least thirty new hosiery plants emerged between 1955 and 1970, many of them small greige-goods companies operated by the owner and consisting of fewer than a dozen employees. Notable in the specialty field was Rampon Products, which fashioned sheer, therapeutic, elastic support stockings under the management of J. M. Ramsay Jr. Beginning in 1960, Rampon fabricated a new type of stocking developed in the firm's own labs, patented and distributed mainly through drugstores. During this period, JRA Industries, also created by Ramsay, began to manufacture elastic yarn.

By 1964 Acme-McCrary alone employed more than fifteen hundred people in six plants. Other established hosiery mills experienced similar upswings. Acme-McCrary had retained its old employees and attracted new ones with the construction, shortly after World War II, of an employees' recreation center, which featured a gymnasium with a basketball court, a cafeteria, an indoor swimming pool, and bowling lanes. Acme-McCrary and Bossong Hosiery Mills also sponsored semi-pro baseball teams in an industrial league. (Acme-McCrary had earlier built the McCrary Ball Park for its industrial league team, the McCrary Eagles. The City of Asheboro Recreation Department later assumed operation of the field, where Asheboro High School and American Legion baseball clubs play their home games.) McCrary also sponsored a semi-pro basketball team that played teams from the University of North Carolina at Chapel Hill, Duke University, and Wake Forest University, as well as top industrial squads.

Another local entrepreneur helped strengthen the county's presence in the furniture industry. Stuart Love formed Stuart Furniture Industries in 1963 to make furniture for mobile homes. The company rapidly expanded into a seven-plant operation and later sold to Klaussner Furniture Industries. Originated in Germany, Klaussner is one of the world's largest furniture manufacturers, and owns and operates retail furniture stores in Europe. The company's corporate offices and main showrooms, however, are in Asheboro. Principal owner Hans Klaussner owns a home at the company-owned Pinewood Country Club, located south of town.

The 1960s and 1970s brought forth two companies in the plastics industry—one company relocating to Randolph County, and the other homegrown. Color Chip Corporation (later renamed Plastic Color-Chips) located a plant in Asheboro to make colorants for plastics. In 1971 Seagrove's Jack Lail opened Mid-State Plastics to fabricate a wide variety of molded plastic products for major companies.

The appearance and further development of new industries gave Randolph workers expanded career choices. It afforded family members more flexibility in choosing their work schedules because the majority of the plants ran two or three eight-hour shifts weekly. Throughout much of the postwar period, area workers benefited from low unemployment rates, while industrial expansion led to competitive wages and generally improved working conditions.

Among these many large, prosperous corporations, one independent business of note flourished as well. During the Great Depression, in 1934, Myrtle Hardin opened a small floral shop in her Liberty home. About eleven years later she built her first greenhouse. (Greenhouses would eventually cover nine acres.) By 1990, Hardin's Wholesale Florist annually produced some three hundred thousand potted plants, including approximately sixty-five thousand poinsettias.

Within this framework of post-World War II enterprise, one Randolphian impacted local commerce and also achieved statewide prominence outside the business arena. Dr. Henry Jordan purchased the old cotton mill and much of the village at Cedar Falls shortly before World War II, converting the facility to manufacture high-quality cotton yarns. Once the war ended and new equipment became available, he updated the facilities and by the mid-1960s employed some two hundred people. Both Dr. Jordan and his brother,

Many speculated Dr. Henry Jordan would become a candidate for governor after gaining statewide notice for directing Gov. W. Kerr Scott's road-building program. However, Jordan declined to bid for the 1954 Democratic Party nomination against Luther Hodges, and later, because of his health, opted not to run for any office. Photograph courtesy of the Randolph County Public Library.

U.S. senator B. Everett Jordan, were born in Ramseur, where their father pastored the local Methodist church.

Henry Jordan was one of three Randolph County men who served as chairman of the state highway commission. Dr. Jordan served one term (1949-1952), industrialist D. B. McCrary served two (1937-1945), and Charles Ross, who joined the highway department staff in 1925 and later was the commission's general counsel, served for about eighteen months in the mid-1940s. Despite this history of leadership and local representation in the highway commission, Randolph continues to rank among the top counties in miles of unpaved secondary roads. Some citizens have interpreted this as punishment for the residents' history of routinely voting the straight Republican Party ticket in a state controlled for much of the century by Democrats.

The years immediately following World War II constituted for Randolph County a period of diversifying the local industrial base and attracting large corporations, whereas the 1950s, 1960s, and 1970s should be recognized for other developments: significant population growth, expanded educational opportunities, the integration of schools and progress in civil rights, the emergence of the arts and other cultural activities, the growth of aviation, and a revival of the Seagrove-area pottery industry. Agriculture, too, remained strong.

By 1950 Randolph County's population had increased to 50,804, up from 36,259 twenty years prior. The 1950 census listed 3,618 farms countywide, with only 1,165 identified as "commercial." A majority of the 27,311 people living on farms were not engaged in commercial farming activities; many simply chose a rural lifestyle and supplemented their incomes and diets with their own produce. A large percentage of part-time farmers held jobs in the public sector. The poultry industry became increasingly attractive to farmers who also held jobs at hosiery mills or furniture factories. Poultry farmers contracted with feed mills or processing plants that guaranteed a fixed price when birds reached certain weights. This vocation did not require the intensive labor of cash crops such as tobacco—the automated delivery of water and feed meant minimal work for the "growers" who could perform their duties in the evening, after their shifts in town. By 1952 tobacco was Randolph's top cash crop, bringing in about $2.5 million of the county's $6 million annual agricultural harvest. (Other crops of significance were corn, wheat, and oats.) Poultry production also expanded and by 1955 matched tobacco's yearly take. Dairy products stood third with $1.5 million in sales, and all other agricultural products totaled $1 million in 1955.

Randolph's population grew from 50,804 in 1950 to 76,356 in 1970. Over this period, most municipalities showed gains: Asheboro, 7,701 to 10,797 (prior to merger with the North Asheboro-Central Falls Sanitary District); Franklinville, 778 to 794; Liberty, 1,342 to 2,167; Ramseur, 1,134 to 1,328; Randleman, 2,066 to 2,312; Seagrove, 319 to 334; and Staley, 236 to 239. Most of the county's population growth occurred in rural areas or in subdivisions located outside incorporated municipalities. Much of the growth can be attributed to people who worked in Greensboro or High Point and lived in Randolph County because of either lower property taxes, the rural environment, or both.

The emergence of educational institutions aided Randolph's growth and contributed skilled workers to local enterprises. Asheboro College, founded in 1949 by Mary Marley and originally called Asheboro Commercial College, was the county's first private business school to open after World War II. Earlene Vestal Ward purchased the school in 1964, and it attracted students from a wide regional area for courses in modern office practices and business machines. In 1948 C. A. Barrett—from 1933 to 1948 the principal of Randolph County Training School (renamed Central High School in 1953), Asheboro's high school for African American students—founded George Washington Carver College. For twelve years the school offered such courses as home management, meal preparation, child care, hotel services, sewing and dressmaking, practical nursing, and business manners.

In the county's public schools, as elsewhere in the nation, the late 1950s brought tension, turmoil, and change. In July 1955 a delegation of black parents—headed by Oscar W. Burwick, an unsuccessful candidate for the Asheboro City Council—petitioned the Asheboro City Board of Education to "take immediate steps to reorganize the public schools . . . on a nondiscriminatory basis." Board chairman Charles W. McCrary appointed a committee of educators and community leaders of both races to recommend to the

C. A. Barrett established George Washington Carver College in 1948 to educate young black students for employment. By 1950 Barrett had acquired land and constructed a modest block building equipped with various teaching tools such as sewing machines and typewriters. Tuition was $40 per year, but donations also supported the school. Courses included home management, catering, child care, practical nursing, and business manners (1954). Photograph courtesy of the Randolph County Public Library.

board how best to implement the 1954 Supreme Court *Brown v. Board of Education* ruling, which stated that separate educational facilities were inherently unequal. However, the *Brown* pronouncement neither specified how best to implement the decision nor did it impose a definite timetable. The resulting white resistance to the court's mandate (particularly in the South) took many forms, some comparatively mild and others violent. Ultimately, school desegregation proved a slow and irregular process, in Randolph County and elsewhere. Meanwhile, in the larger 1950s civil rights arena, at least one local establishment opened its doors to blacks. In November 1955, the municipal golf course accepted its first African American golfers without incident.

In August 1962, parents of twenty-two black students requested assignment to the all-white Trinity Unity School. Only fourteen of these students showed up for reassignment hearings. In August 1963, there were several days of unrest in Asheboro because of resistance to integration, and police issued twenty-nine arrest warrants on charges ranging from engaging in an affray (primarily fist-fights) to loitering to public drunkenness. The turmoil continued when police arrested eleven white men, on charges of trespassing, amidst bumper-to-bumper downtown traffic and a mob of sidewalk onlookers and hecklers.

In January 1964, local black leaders called for "silent march" demonstrations to protest racial discrimination. On the first night 101 marched, but on the following night the number dwindled to 68 marchers, all of them black. Integration of dining establishments, however, proved anything but peaceful. Civil rights demonstrations occurred on several occasions in downtown Asheboro when young African Americans attempted to be served in booths or counters at restaurants. Denied service, they protested by staging sit-down demonstrations both inside and on the sidewalks outside the establishments. The protesters blocked entryways until policemen hauled them away. District courts found five demonstrators guilty of trespassing and issued thirty-day sentences, suspended upon good behavior and payment of fifty-dollar fines. Defendants appealed. In a separate incident, two NAACP officers announced in February 1964 that they would suffocate themselves in coffins in downtown Asheboro unless public schools were desegregated by May 30. This demonstration failed to materialize, but a number of curious onlookers and would-be hecklers showed up. In August, upon parents' request, the school board reassigned four black students to the all-white Lindley Park School. By the autumn of 1965, all schools in both the city and county school systems were desegregated. In the county system, officials drew new district lines, closed three schools for blacks (including one brand-new high school in Liberty), and planned for four new integrated high schools.

Randolph Industrial Education Center (RIEC), now Randolph Community College, admitted its first students in 1962, with day and evening classes in such fields as accounting, automotive mechanics, business administration, floral design, welding, office technology, photography, secretarial science, and a host of other courses, according to demand. The Asheboro-Randolph Chamber of Commerce and the college widely advertised throughout the industrial community that the college was eager to offer new courses to train workers for area industries. This resource helped recruit new companies to the county. The campus sits within Randolph's industrial park, where several of the new industries, including Rampon Products, JRA Industries, Bost Neckwear, Richard Grey Hosiery, and Potter Manufacturing, located in the late 1960s.

Just prior to World War II, a group of businessmen had built a landing field at this location in south Asheboro. (Randolph County commissioners acquired the property for development of an industrial park, later the site of Randolph Community College.) However, the history of aviation in the county actually dates to the late 1920s, when Teak Presnell and Gordon H. York, Asheboro High School students, purchased the first airplane in Randolph County in 1929 (a Curtis JN4D "Jenny"). The absence of airfields relegated them to taking off and landing in cow pastures. In August 1960 the City of Asheboro, seeking the expansion of aviation, purchased a 196-acre former dairy farm located southwest of town on N.C. 49 with plans to construct the Asheboro Municipal Airport there. The airport opened in September 1965, and in the late 1990s the primary runway was expanded to fifty-five hundred feet, making it capable of handling 90 percent of general aviation and small-jet traffic.

Another area of mid-century development included cultural establishments and activities, and the arts. Randolph County could boast of having one of the oldest continuing historical societies in the state, organized in the autumn of 1911. Townspeople organized history museums in Randleman and Archdale. Prior to Dwight M. Holland becoming the first art teacher in the Asheboro public schools in 1954 and organizing the first children's art exhibit, the arts had failed to flourish in Randolph. In 1973 Jerry Jones became the county's first director of cultural arts, and he emphasized the visual arts, drama, and music programs in the county schools. Eleven years earlier, Randolph Community College had begun offering day and evening art classes.

In 1973 Dwight Holland, enthusiastic over the success of fall festivals held in other parts of the state, organized the annual Randolph Fall Festival to feature the fruits of the harvest and showcase the works of local artists, such as baskets, pottery, paintings, woodcrafts, quilts, and blacksmithing. The festival has continued uninterrupted, attracting an estimated fifty to one hundred thousand people on the first weekend of October. Adding to the celebration have been

Pictured here are the Bicentennial Costume winners at the 1976 Randolph Fall Festival. Photograph courtesy of the Randolph County Public Library.

performers such as cloggers, folk dancers, fiddlers, gospel and bluegrass musicians, and an assortment of foods ranging from barbecue to hand-churned ice cream.

These and other activities spearheaded the establishment of the Randolph Arts Guild. In 1989 the Arts Guild purchased a building in downtown Asheboro and established the W. H. Moring Jr. Arts Center, utilizing generous financial support from Moring's grand-daughter, Marion Moring Stedman Covington. The Moring Center, with a full-time director, staff, crafts shop, and art galleries, continues to sponsor year-round art exhibits, mainly featuring local artists. The center offers arts and crafts lessons for all ages with a small core of staff, visiting artists, and teachers. Classes offered include painting in various media, sculpture, music, wood carving, and writing.

The pottery revival in the Seagrove area began with the 1921 establishment of Jugtown Pottery by Jacques and Juliana Busbee. After this development, more than a half century passed before many of the progeny of the early potters returned to the trade their families had abandoned during an era when the production of inexpensive tin and enamel containers undercut the business and forced artisans to take factory jobs or concentrate on farming. In the intervening years, some who still had a potter's wheel stored away in a shed came to recognize that the traditional pottery industry had been redefined with Oriental themes and had created a market for decorative items, as opposed to only the traditional and utilitarian. Over the years, potters had discovered that bog clay—which was heavy with iron— gave their wares a distinctive darker hue, and that the pond at Holly Spring produced clay of a much lighter color. This material was well suited for experimenting with new glazes to augment the salt and alkaline dips of long tradition. By 1969 some potters had realized that selling pottery in their own shops was more rewarding (both personally and financially) than shipping pots to shops catering to the tourist trade.

In 1969 Walter and Dorothy Cole Auman, descendants of early potters, opened Seagrove Potters Museum in the abandoned Seagrove train depot, which they moved to a location behind their pottery workshop and salesroom on U.S. 220 at the northern limits of Seagrove. This old Aberdeen and Asheboro Railroad depot had seen many pots shipped from its docks over the years and at its new location displayed a documented collection of North Carolina pottery from the eighteenth and nineteenth centuries, as well as works by

Dorothy Cole Auman fashions a piece of pottery in her Seagrove workshop. A native of Moore County, N.C., Auman, and her husband, Walter, co-founded the Seagrove Potters Museum. The Aumans died in a 1991 car accident. Photograph courtesy of the Randolph County Public Library.

contemporary traditional potters. By 1976 there were a total of eleven potters selling from their own shops in the Seagrove area, offering both traditional and contemporary wares of their own ingenuity and creativity. Other potteries operating at this time included Cole's Pottery, run by Nell Cole Graves and Waymon Cole; Joe Owens Shop; M. L. Owens Pottery, with Boyd Owens, proprietor; and Jugtown, run by Nancy Sweezy, her husband Hobart, and her father Duck Teague (who purchased the business that had changed hands several times after the death of Juliana Busbee in 1947). Studio potters were also busy: Bob Armfield at Coleridge, Phillip Pollet at Old Gap Pottery, Phil Morgan at Steeds, Jerry Fenburg at Humble Mills, and Phil Pugh at Salem. These artisans regularly enticed hordes of visitors, and budding young potters found this congregation of potters an especially appealing place to learn and to display their own talents.

Along with the revival of the local pottery trade, the last half of the twentieth century saw both the arrival and the departure of a number of newspapers. The stability of this industry in Randolph County, as in most other locales, has faced threats from keen competition and consolidation among the print media, television, radio, the Internet, and other electronic media. The *Randolph Guide*, a weekly established in 1953 by Paul Cutright and acquired two years later by L. Barron Mills Jr., was purchased in January 1991 by Robert Derr, who, one year later, acquired the *Ramseur Bulletin* from the Pell family. In 1994 Derr bought the *Randleman Reporter*, which was established in the 1980s, from Womack Publishing Company. Community Newspaper Holdings purchased all three from Derr on October 27, 1999, and shortly thereafter their circulation lists were merged with the *Randolph Guide*.

The *Courier-Tribune,* meanwhile, had changed from a semiweekly to a six-days-a-week afternoon newspaper and also changed ownership twice. In June 2000, the Greensboro-based *News and Record*, owned by Landmark Publications of Norfolk, Virginia, announced it was establishing a bureau in Asheboro. The bureau was to be staffed with reporters and advertising and circulation personnel. The *Courier-Tribune*, published in Asheboro and owned by Donrey Media Group headquartered in Las Vegas, Nevada, announced it was converting into a daily morning newspaper and adding a Saturday edition. Long gone are all of the other newspapers that had dotted the county over the years: the *Liberty Register* (1898-1900), the *Liberty Herald* (1894), the Liberty *Villager* (1981-ca. 1982), the *Randleman News* (dates unknown), *Political Broadaxe* (1890), the *Randleman Blazer* (1896), and *The Randolphian* (1946-1949). Newspaper publisher Roy Cox Sr. and industrialist W. Clyde Lucas were granted a license in 1947 for the first radio station in Randolph, which was followed in 1971 by a second AM station organized by a group of area businessmen.

Various groups have developed properties or promoted attractions in Randolph County that draw visitors. In 1962 the Thomasville District of the United Methodist Church purchased land on Mount Shepherd to develop a youth camp and conference center. In that same year, the Baptist State Convention built Camp Caraway (named for a portion of the Uwharrie range) for boys, then constructed Camp Mundo Vista for girls in 1969, and at Caraway developed a year-round conference center with lodging and dining facilities that continue to attract many groups from across the state.

The Asheboro-Randolph Chamber of Commerce has sought to attract groups and individuals to the county. Organized in the mid-1920s, it took a prominent role in forming the Randolph Tourist Development Bureau, an organization funded entirely by a special tax on lodging receipts. The bureau began operations in the late 1990s and hired a director to promote the county's many tourist attractions. These included the North Carolina Pottery Center and individual potteries, the North Carolina Aviation Museum at the Asheboro airport, the Richard Petty Museum at Randleman, the American Classic Motorcycle Museum in Asheboro, Richland Creek Herb and Flower Farm, the numerous antique and art galleries in Asheboro, the Liberty Antiques Festival (held every April and September and attracting some four hundred dealers), the Rand Ol' Opry music hall in Ramseur, Caraway Speedway (a short track on the NASCAR Weekly Racing Series), and NASCAR Day Festival, an event that attracts drivers, vendors, and race fans to Randleman every August.

Randolph County's central location in the state was a deciding factor in 1969 and 1970 when the North Carolina Jaycees and the

North Carolina Zoological Park and Botanical Gardens, respectively, chose county sites for their operations. The Jaycees deemed land on Country Club Drive, donated by the City of Asheboro, an ideal site for their state headquarters; that the Asheboro Municipal Golf Course sat adjacent factored nicely into the equation. The group constructed a building to house the offices of the Jaycees' state headquarters and executive secretary, and to host state board meetings and other functions.

In October 1971 the Randolph County Society for Zoological Development donated to the state 1,371 acres of land on Purgatory Mountain in Grant Township to develop the country's "largest walk-through natural habitat zoo." World-renowned zoo authorities had proclaimed that the property, though hilly, reminded them of the African plains. Local citizens donated funds to purchase the land during a campaign headed by attorney D. Wescott Moser and industrialist W. David Stedman of Asheboro. North Carolinians approved a $2 million bond issue for the zoo's design and development, and Randolph County approved $1.8 million to

Gazelles gather together in a North Carolina Zoo exhibit. Photograph courtesy of the Randolph County Public Library.

The curatorial staff at the North Carolina Zoological Park devised a way to create artificial rocks that resemble Randolph County's indigenous rock formations. In this photograph of the zoo under construction, a worker is fabricating the rocks, which serve as barriers or for housing the animals. Photograph courtesy of the Randolph County Public Library.

extend water and sewer lines to the site. J. Hyatt Hammond Associates of Asheboro developed a master plan for its design, and the Z. Smith Reynolds Foundation granted $1 million, which the General Assembly matched. All told, the Randolph County and state governments, citizens, industries, and charitable foundations initially donated more than $16 million for the North Carolina Zoological Park and Botanical Gardens. The first phase of the permanent zoo opened in late 1979.

Democrats have historically outnumbered Republicans on the county's voter registration books, but the figures belie how the citizenry voted. Many Republicans have registered as Democrats in order to qualify to vote in the Democratic Party primaries. Because their party had few local primaries, Republicans needed to take this step in order to have a voice in who represented them in state and federal government. As late as 1964, when the county's registered voters numbered 24,384, Democratic registrations totaled 13,072 and Republican registrations 10,555, with 757 declaring themselves "independent." However, by 1984, with a total voter registration of 51,254, Republicans outnumbered Democrats by 730; there were 2,560 "unaffiliated" and 8 Libertarians on the registration rolls.

Russell Grady Walker, for three decades the most recognizable Randolph County Democrat in the state, served on the Asheboro City Council from 1961 to 1965 and was elected to the state senate in 1975. Area voters reelected him five times. He served as chairman of the North Carolina Democratic Party from 1975 to 1981. Walker managed Congressman Nick Galifianakis's 1972 campaign against Jesse Helms in the latter's first campaign for the U.S. Senate. Helms and his campaign manager, Raleigh attorney Tom Ellis, devised Helms's campaign slogan, "He's one of us," portraying Galifianakis, son of a Greek immigrant, as an outsider.

The Watergate incident of 1974 helped elect Democrats to the county commission. Many local Republicans proclaimed their disgust over the actions of President Richard Nixon and the Watergate fiasco by voting for Democrats. In fact, Democrats became chairmen of the commission for the first time in about thirty years, with J. Logan White serving as chair from 1974 to 1975, and 1977 to 1978, and Frank Auman Jr. serving from 1975 to 1977. Matilda Phillips of Liberty became the first female and the century's last Democratic commissioner in 1976.

In 1970 Asheboro attorney John Randolph Ingram became the first Democrat chosen to represent Randolph and Montgomery counties in the North Carolina House of Representatives. Two years later, voters elected him state commissioner of insurance, then reelected him in 1976. Ingram thus became the second Randolphian to hold this office—Waldo Cheek, also a Democrat, had won a 1949 appointment to the post, in order to fill a vacancy, and voters elected him in 1950 and in 1952. Ingram was among eight candidates in the 1978 Democratic primary for the U.S. Senate, and in the second primary he defeated Luther Hodges Jr. (the former governor's namesake) by a vote of 244,469 to 206,223. In the general election, incumbent senator Jesse Helms defeated Ingram 619,151 to 516,663. Randolph County voters chose Helms 12,583 to 7,796. Helms's organization outspent Ingram's thirty to one in garnering 56 percent of the total vote.

In 1995 Harold James Brubaker of Randolph County, active in the state Republican organization, became North Carolina's Speaker of the House, the first Republican selected to this post since Reconstruction. He was first elected in 1977 and has continued to serve for fourteen consecutive terms. Brubaker served as Speaker of the House for two terms. A former teacher, he is president of a real estate appraisal firm. He served as chairman of the Randolph County Young Republicans and the North Carolina Republican Party's executive committee. He served on the joint caucus committee in the state house and also as minority leader. In the state senate, Betsy Lane Cochrane, born and reared in Asheboro, has been a longtime leader of the Republican Party, serving as minority leader, minority whip, and delegate to the national GOP convention, plus many other leadership roles. First elected in 1989, she lives in Davie County and represented the Thirty-eighth District until 2000 when she became a candidate for lieutenant governor, an election she lost.

The last half of the twentieth century brought a new generation of Randolph leaders on the state scene. It was a period of remarkable industrial growth in the county, bringing new companies, diversification, and business mergers. Randolphians witnessed the complete integration of public schools and public facilities. Advancements occurred in adult education, the arts, and tourism, all greatly enhanced by the arrival of the North Carolina Zoo and the burgeoning pottery trade.

Epilogue

*M*oving into the twenty-first century, there appeared on the horizon a bright future in virtually every sector of Randolph County's growth. The county population in 2000 stood at 130,672, compared with 106,546 in 1990 and 91,728 in 1980. Asheboro's 2000 population numbered 21,672, a growth of 32 percent (some 5,000 residents) in ten years, with an appreciable number of Hispanics accounting for much of the gain. The year 2000 populations and the 1990 figures (in parentheses) of the county's other incorporated towns were: Archdale, 9,014 (6,913); Liberty, 2,661 (2,049); Franklinville, 1,258 (666); Ramseur, 1,588 (1,186); Randleman, 3,557 (2,612); Seagrove, 246 (244); Staley, 347 (204); and Trinity, 6,690 (not incorporated until 1997). Both Seagrove and Staley experienced population losses in the 1980s.

By the twenty-first century, Archdale had become the second-most populous municipality in the county, largely by attracting citizens who commute to Guilford County to work. Archdale also became the second-largest town in acreage: nearly twenty square miles. At the turn of the twenty-first century, Seagrove remained the only incorporated town in the southern half of Randolph; its thriving pottery enterprises are bringing renewed vitality.

By the late 1900s, Randolph had more Quaker congregations (twelve, with a membership of about three thousand) than any other county in the state, including Guilford County, which had only five. Asheboro's St. Joseph's Catholic, the town's only Catholic church, added new services, including Masses in Spanish on Saturdays and Sundays. The Methodist Church assigned a Spanish-speaking pastor to Asheboro and helped establish a new church.

In the local political milieu, registered Republicans outnumbered Democrats 42,602 to 21,758, as of March 2007. Unaffiliated registrants numbered 15,776.

Despite the recent growth of municipalities, Randolph County remains largely rural in character, and agriculture has continued to play a significant role in the county's economy. Whereas tobacco and poultry constituted the chief cash crops in 1952—each accounting for about $2.5 million of the county's $6 million in farm income—by 1997 the value of farm products totaled $147.3 million, with livestock sales accounting for 90 percent and field crops 10 percent. By 2004, cash receipts for agriculture in Randolph were $212,003,000, placing it ninth in the state. It ranked seventh in livestock, dairy and poultry, and thirty-fourth in crops. Agricultural production is expected to remain strong, especially if the trend toward job losses in the textile industry persists. The tables below give more detail regarding specific crops and livestock.

Randolph County Crop Statistics (2005)

Crops (2005)	Acres Harv.	Yield	Production	State Rank
Tobacco, Lbs.	64	2,273	1,455,000	39
Cotton, 480 Lb. bales	*	*	*	*
Soybeans, Bu.	9,700	33	321,000	40
Corn, Bu.	5,400	119	640,000	39
Corn for silage, Tons	2,600	14	36,100	6
Peanuts, Lbs.	*	*	*	*
Small grains:				
Wheat, Bu.	4,000	55	220,000	29
Barley, Bu.	*	*	*	*
Oats, Bu.	450	67	30,000	20
Sweet potatoes, Cwt.	*	*	*	*
Irish potatoes, Cwt.	*	*	*	*
All hay, Tons	19,500	2.46	47,900	4
Sorghum, Bu.	*	*	*	*

Randolph County Livestock Statistics (2005)

Livestock	Number	State Rank
Hogs and pigs (Dec. 1, 2005)	25,000	33
Cattle (Jan. 1, 2006)	37,000	2
Beef cows (Jan. 1, 2006)	16,500	1
Milk cows (Jan. 1, 2006)	2,500	3
Broilers produced (2005)	46,000,000	3
Turkeys raised (2005)	*	*
All chickens (Dec. 1, 2005)	1,140,000	6

NOTE: If fewer than 200 acres of a crop are harvested in a county, the statistics are not published and are designated by an asterisk (*). Likewise, fewer than 500,000 broilers or turkeys raised are designated by an asterisk. SOURCE: The North Carolina Department of Agriculture and Consumer Services.

Among the county's long-standing non-agricultural enterprises, three of the families who founded the largest hosiery companies—the McCrary-Reddings, Cranfords, and Bossongs—continued to head the same companies into the third and fourth generations, despite strong competition from hosiery manufacturers in Japan and elsewhere. Members of the Page family continue to operate P&P Chair Company, which dates from 1926.

Textiles and furniture manufacturing—long the linchpins of commerce in Randolph County—began to take on lesser economic roles in the twenty-first century, as high-tech industries requiring specially trained employees began to make inroads. This development contributed to Randolph becoming the only county in the Piedmont Triad region to show a growing population, especially in the twenty-five to thirty age group. In Randleman, Liberty, and elsewhere, the development of industrial parks and multipurpose shell buildings to attract new businesses has engendered optimism. Randolph Community College geared up to expand its technological training facilities. Many hoped that attracting high-tech companies would soon elevate the county's poor showing in average weekly manufacturing wages: $599.00, compared with a state average of $832.00 in 2007, and nearby Guilford's $865.00 and Forsyth's $1,127.00.

As of January 2007, 42 percent of the county's work force of 76,846 was engaged in the manufacturing sector. Klaussner Furniture Industries, the largest privately owned company in the United States, employed over thirty-nine hundred area workers, more than any other private company. Other furniture manufacturers included Hughes Furniture Industries, United Furniture, and March Furniture Manufacturing; relatedly, Hafele America Company produced furniture hardware.

Beyond these furniture manufacturers, a list of the county's top employers in early 2007 showed much diversity. Textiles were represented by four companies: Ramtex, producing synthetic fabrics; Kayser-Roth, fabricating nylon and cotton socks; Wells Hosiery, making hosiery; and Acme-McCrary, making women's activewear and intimate apparel. Other industries (and their products) making the list were batteries at Energizer Battery; molded plastics at Technimark; plastic cups and lids at Dart Container; mattresses at

Sealy; catheters at Arrow International; medical pantyhose at Elastic Therapy; wire for radial truck tires at Goodyear Tire and Rubber; rubber products at Oliver Rubber; foam products at Prestige Fabricators; kitchen and bathroom cabinets at UltraCraft; and high-precision roller bearings at The Timken Company. Wal-Mart was the only retail store on the list. The top education, government, and health-care employers were Randolph County Schools, Asheboro City Schools, the County of Randolph, the City of Asheboro, and Randolph Hospital.

In recent years, and for reasons beyond the scope of this book to examine, the county's manufacturing sector has waned, resulting in job losses. The Cranford family has closed its Asheboro Hosiery Mills. In June 2001, 170 workers at Caraway Furniture in Sophia lost their jobs when the plant closed. Several other furniture plants experienced significant layoffs around that time, and it is unclear whether these losses are permanent and a harbinger of future trends. Textiles also suffered local losses when Galey and Lord—one of the first Klopman Industries plants in 1947, later merging with Burlington Industries—closed its doors to 120 employees in 2001. The Black and Decker small-appliance plant, acquired by Windmere Holdings, ceased operations in 1999. Cooper Tire and Rubber leased a portion of the building for a tire distribution center that relocated from Athens, Georgia. The B. B. Walker Company, faced with bankruptcy, closed its last remaining shoe plant and its Asheboro retail store in early 2002. Luck's, the food-processing company owned by American Home Products and employing 120, was acquired in August 2001 by ConAgra Grocery Products. Within a year, ConAgra closed the Seagrove plant in order to consolidate production in California. More recently, Unilever moved its production operations to Canada in 2006, costing 240 jobs.

This type of action has become increasingly common in Randolph, as elsewhere in the country, when large corporations desire to reduce production costs by pursuing consolidations and mergers. However, other companies' recent expansions have helped offset this trend somewhat: in 2005, StarPet announced an expansion in Asheboro, creating forty new jobs; and a Timken expansion was expected to add fifty new jobs.

Despite a recent rash of layoffs and job losses, the county as a whole has continued to prosper, necessitating a continual expansion of municipal services. By the mid-1900s, the Randolph County Courthouse, dedicated in 1909, was judged inadequate to accommodate all of the courts and related offices. The county built three additions between the early 1950s and the early 1980s. Cramped for space in 1980, the county constructed a new office complex and named it in honor of longtime county commissioner Ira L. McDowell. It sits on county-owned property in south Asheboro, behind the old vacant county home for the indigent, elderly, and handicapped. In less than a decade, additional growing pains spurred the county to purchase, from the new owners of the Stedman Corporation, an almost-new corporate office building on McDowell Road. A new jail was soon built on this same tract, replacing the one built almost a century prior, and the sheriff's department moved to the county office building. In 1996 county commissioners introduced plans for a new courthouse complex containing seven new courtrooms and ancillary facilities, a new facade and entrance on Salisbury Street, adequate parking, and security screening. As part of the project, the 1909 courthouse roof was replaced, and the building's exterior weather-conditioned for protection. The total capitalized cost for the new courthouse building alone was a little over $13,345,000. In 2002, staff began moving into the updated complex, which houses seven courtrooms and various offices, including the Randolph County Clerk of Court, the Randolph County District Attorney, and district and superior court judges.

An associate member of the Randolph Arts Guild, the RSVP Community Theatre produces at least three shows a year—one of which is a large scale musical—by utilizing funds from ticket sales, sponsorships, and donations. In the past, the Guild held free summer concerts in downtown Asheboro's Bicentennial Park, but the City of Asheboro has been the producer of the series since 2005. Among its many activities, the Guild sponsors a large fall festival, a popular annual event for more than thirty years, and the North Carolina Potters Conference. These events help draw visitors downtown, where antique shops dominate Sunset Avenue. A number of retailers—a few of them formerly located downtown—relocated to

The new Randolph County Courthouse provided much-needed modernized courtroom and office space. Displayed in the courthouse is a collection of historical photographs from each of the county's townships. Photograph by Paul Church and courtesy of the *Courier-Tribune*.

Randolph Mall and to strip shopping centers. Among these outlying retailers, Kmart closed its Asheboro store (the only one in Randolph) as it fought to escape bankruptcy.

Among the county's media, one daily and two weekly newspapers continue: the *Courier-Tribune*, owned by Stephens Media Group; the *Archdale-Trinity News*, owned by the *High Point Enterprise*; and the *Randolph Guide*, owned by Community Newspaper Holdings of Alabama. The *Liberty News*, which was owned by the *Chatham News* in Siler City, ceased publication in 2003. The only hospital in the county at the turn of the twenty-first century was Asheboro's Randolph Hospital, which opened in 1932. In recent years, the hospital has greatly expanded its scope of operations and has located satellite physicians' offices in other parts of the county.

Two relics of the Civil War are still extant, in addition to the Confederate monument on the courthouse lawn. The Asheborough Female Academy, which on occasion housed Confederate troops, has been preserved. The Randolph Hornets' banner, carried in the Civil War by Company M, Twenty-second Regiment, North Carolina Troops, currently is displayed in the Randolph County Historical Society's collection at the Asheboro Public Library. A structure of historical interest is the Marmaduke Swaim Robins law office, a two-room wooden building built about 1860. It is the last surviving building on Asheboro's nineteenth-century courthouse square. After Marmaduke's death, the building became the office of his son, lawyer Henry Moring Robins, and served as Asheboro's first town hall when Robins was mayor from 1907 to 1909. It has been moved a short distance from its original site to property owned by the City of Asheboro, and the Randolph County Bar Association has helped preserve the structure.

The construction of highways has profoundly impacted the county in recent decades. New interstate highways, currently in the developmental stages, will almost certainly bring forth great change. Officials expect Randolph County to gain widespread recognition and tourist dollars from thousands of new visitors when each of the currently temporary segments of interstate highways I-73 and I-74 meets the necessary standards, routing travelers through the county from as far away as Canada and the Midwest. The two interstates will utilize many existing roadways, including the segments of four-laned U.S. 220 from Randleman to Candor. Already completed in a number of midwestern states, I-74 will enter the Tar Heel State from Virginia near Mount Airy, North Carolina, then pass through Winston-Salem, High Point, and Randleman. No definite timetable has been established for bringing all segments of the highways up to interstate standards, and only then will the full local impact of these highways be felt. The two new interstate highways extend north to Sault Ste. Marie, Michigan, at the United States-Canada border. These interstates will connect there with Trans Canada Highways 11 and 17, the main highways in Canada. Under current proposals, both I-73 and I-74 will pass into South Carolina near Rockingham and Wilmington, North Carolina, respectively, and terminate somewhere near Myrtle Beach, South Carolina.

The interstate corridor is expected to result in the establishment of new restaurants and lodging, perhaps persuading travelers to linger in Randolph and visit the area's attractions, notably the North Carolina Zoo. Asheboro gained a new K&W Cafeteria in late 2001, largely because of the anticipated new highways. Some Randleman residents had hoped to take advantage of this influx of visitors by legalizing the sale of liquor, beer, and wine with meals, but a 2001 referendum failed to pass the measure. Randleman's ABC liquor store, and other licensed beer and wine retailers, have sold their products (for off-premises consumption only) since 1965. Liberty remains the only municipality in the county with on-premises and off-premises sales of beer, and the town also supports an ABC store. Asheboro voters routinely turn down proposals to establish ABC stores and off-premises sales of beer and wine. The most recent referendum, conducted in 1994, upheld the town's status as the largest legally dry municipality in North Carolina.

In addition to new roads and various developments, Randolph County leaders have formulated plans for other infrastructure. A significant new water source addresses the Piedmont Triad region's ever-present water problems. In the mid-1930s the U.S. Army Corps of Engineers launched a Randleman dam and lake project for Deep River and Cape Fear River basin flood control and water conservation. The corps, after creating B. Everett Jordan Lake in Chatham County, later abandoned the venture. However, the Randleman lake project resumed upon the formation of the Piedmont Triad Regional Water Authority (PTRWA), which area counties organized to provide treated water for Greensboro, High Point, Jamestown, Archdale, Randleman, Asheboro, and unspecified areas in Randolph County.

The clearing of land for the lake, and the construction of a concrete and earthen dam one hundred feet high and seventy feet across, began in 2001. Organizers expect the impoundment to provide a daily yield of forty-eight million gallons of water from a three-thousand-acre lake. The dam sits just north of Randleman High School, and the lake bed stretches into the southern part of Guilford County. Construction, land acquisition, and other costs for the lake and dam have been estimated at $124 million. Asheboro opted not to join the consortium because it benefits from surplus water drawn from a series of lakes built at intervals since the 1930s. These lakes also furnish water to the North Carolina Zoological Park and Botanical Gardens, and a metered pipeline to Randleman provides an alternate supply when the town's municipal reservoir is low. Members of the Piedmont Triad Regional Water Authority consortium are the County of Randolph, Randleman, Archdale, Jamestown, High Point, and Greensboro. All of these agencies will be able to tap into the lake's pipelines. In December 2006 the

PTRWA Board proceeded with a plan for a sixty-million-dollar water treatment plant that will treat water from the recently completed reservoir project. If all members agree to fund their share of the construction costs, treated water from Randleman Lake could be available by 2011.

Randolph's new highways, water sources, and other infrastructure and developments are products of the county's prosperity and growth. These creations, correspondingly antecedents to and by-products of growth, have also helped transform the local economy, one in which tourism and services now augment the county's traditional industries. A new youth camp, an expansion of the vintage aircraft museum at Asheboro Municipal Airport (North Carolina Aviation Museum), the promotion and marketing of the pottery industry, and the hiring of a new tourism director have drawn attention to Randolph County. The local tourist bureau envisions a new tourism center to offer visitors information and a rest stop.

The North Carolina Zoological Park's North American and African continents have been redesigned, with some five hundred

The early-1980s opening of the pavilion area at the North Carolina Zoological Park and Botanical Gardens drew large crowds. Photograph courtesy of the Randolph County Public Library.

acres of exhibits and trails and more than one thousand animals. Other zoo features include Discovery Center—designed to study the interconnectedness of life—shops, restaurants, walks, trails to exhibits, a tram and bus system with easy access for the disabled, shuttle parking, and other amenities. Dr. David Jones, the former director of the London Zoo, became director in the late 1990s. His master plan includes a motel and convention center complex and the development of other features to make visitors want to spend more time in Randolph County, visiting the state zoo and other attractions. The plan encompasses points of interest such as the last remaining covered bridge in Randolph County, the Pisgah Covered Bridge. In what could have been a disastrous loss, on August 9, 2003, the bridge was washed away by heavy rains to approximately fifty yards downstream. Dr. Jones recruited volunteers to scour the countryside along the stream to recover parts and stray lumber, and return the bridge to its former location. The volunteers also visited old barns and stables in the county to get planks and other materials to repair the structure. New footings were built and beams reinforced as the bridge was elevated to protect it from future flooding.

Pisgah Covered Bridge, shown here just after it was washed away by heavy rainwater, was later rebuilt. Photograph by Erika Crocker.

Public funds and private donations covered the costs of the restoration, and the bridge was rededicated in May 2004.

In 1999 the wonders of Ridges Mountain, in the Uwharrie chain, captured the attention of the Piedmont Land Conservancy, a nonprofit land trust that seeks to purchase some 136 acres to protect the area's natural beauty and preserve its distinctive wildlife habitats and its "fun places to explore and climb." A mature forest and giant boulders not found elsewhere in the state make Ridges Mountain unique. Also, the land supports endangered flora and aquatic life in and around upland depression pools. Director Jones's plan calls for the North Carolina Zoological Park and Botanical Gardens to take charge of the site once the Conservancy acquires it.

In 2000 the Petty family, known for its longtime success on the NASCAR racing circuit, unveiled plans to develop Victory Junction Gang Camp for children with chronic and life-threatening illnesses. Kyle and Pattie Petty revealed the plans, patterned after and associated with the Paul Newman Hole in the Wall Gang Camps. Promoters conducted a fund-raising drive, soliciting donations from foundations, corporations, and individuals. The seventy-two-acre site

Racing legend Richard Petty poses next to his race car at the Opening Festival for the North Carolina Museum of History in 1994. The car is on display at the North Carolina Sports Hall of Fame. Photograph courtesy of the North Carolina Museum of History.

on Fred Lineberry Road in Randolph County's Level Cross community was donated by Richard and Linda Petty. The first campers attended in June 2004. Supported by ongoing fund-raising activities, Victory Junction offers free sessions to participants and their families. Most attendees come from North Carolina, South Carolina, and Virginia, but approximately 15 percent come from other parts of the country.

Seagrove, one of Randolph County's primary tourist destinations, is undeniably the pottery capital of the state. An influx of studio potters has joined traditional potters, forging ahead with new innovations and ideas, making Seagrove one of the largest and oldest communities of working potters in the United States. Residents hope to spawn more interest and attract more visitors to the town and the pottery community, which extends into neighboring counties. In 1979 there were only eleven pottery shops displaying their wares. By 2001 the number approached one hundred, demonstrating a diversity of styles and techniques ranging from utilitarian stoneware to delicate, intricate, and ornamental works of art. Many of the craftsmen are eighth- or ninth-generation potters.

Two pottery museums are in ongoing stages of development. The year 1992 brought the organization of the North Carolina Pottery Center; work was completed and a director hired in 1998. The museum is governed by a board composed of potters, collectors, and supporters from across the state. The center features a permanent exhibit that traces the development of pottery in North Carolina, from the early Native Americans to the present. More than two hundred pieces of pottery, artifacts, and photographs document the emergence of the pottery trade. Exhibits cover topics on historical and contemporary works. Visiting artists give lectures and demonstrations, and examples of different types of kilns are on the premises. The Museum of North Carolina Traditional Pottery, located in the Seagrove town hall but slated to move into the old Seagrove Grocery building, focuses its attention on promoting Seagrove-area potters. It sponsors the Seagrove Pottery Festival on the weekend before Thanksgiving at Seagrove School. In recent festivals, over seventy potters each year display and sell their best works. A commemorative pottery item is always offered for sale.

Once a pottery museum, the Seagrove train depot ceased to be such in October 1991 when Walter and Dorothy Auman, who had

Shoppers browse the many beautiful offerings at the North Carolina Pottery Center (1998). Photograph by the author.

moved the building to adjoin their pottery shop on U.S. 220, died in an auto accident. (Their pottery collection was subsequently donated to a museum.) A few years ago, proposals were made to move the Seagrove train depot back to a site near its original location and develop it as a transportation museum. Suggestions included exhibits recalling the days of the plank road, which passed through the county, and the railroads, which shipped large quantities of crossties and pottery items from this location. These proposals, however, have yet to be pursued, and the depot's future is uncertain. Potters, promoters, and developers of all these museums share the common goals of promoting pottery and Seagrove as a destination.

Typical of the young potters following in the Seagrove tradition is Ben Owen III, who received his first lessons from his grandfather, Ben Owen, who left Jugtown Pottery after the death of Juliana Busbee and opened Old Plank Road Pottery in 1972. In the mid–1970s, young Ben's hands were guided by those of his grandfather, who suffered from crippling arthritis. The grandfather taught the youngster the value of keeping shapes and designs simple. The elder Owen closed the shop in 1972, and his son, B. Wade Owen Jr., reopened it a year later as Ben Owen Pottery, located in the Westmore community just south of the Randolph border. He hoped to encourage his son to pursue pottery as a career. Ben III has built upon the family tradition and has experimented with designs from other cultures, including neolithic Chinese and African forms and those from the southwestern United States. He began throwing pots at age thirteen and believes "it is a challenge to work with clay. Clay gives you a chance to be expressive." Owen appreciates the early forms of pots and enjoys experimenting with new forms. Chinese red is his favorite color for pottery. Owen's work and that of many other potters of the Westmore area show a German as well as an English influence. Ben III has built a new home and shop in the Westmore community, and in 2004, he was honored as a North Carolina Living Treasure, a prestigious award for creative excellence presented by the University of North Carolina at Wilmington's Museum of World Cultures.

Sixteen-month-old Avery Owen likes this piece of pottery swiftly taking shape under the skillful hands of her father, Ben Owen III, at the Ben Owen Pottery on Route 2, Seagrove, in the Westmore area. Avery is being held by her mother, LoriAnn Little Owen (2002). Ben was recently honored by the North Carolina Living Treasures project, one of the highest honors given by the state to honor creative excellence. Photograph by the author.

In addition to the pottery community and its museums, another local museum—this one at the Asheboro Municipal Airport—also has been actively seeking widespread recognition. The North Carolina Aviation Museum, founded and initially funded by Jim Pettycord as a manifestation of his interest in World War II "warbirds," has been nurtured for more than a decade by the Pettycord Foundation for Aircraft Conservation. Pettycord, owner of MatLab (a plastics and metals finishing company), and his son, Rick, an Air Force pilot, lost their lives when the two vintage planes they were flying clipped wings and crashed in the Grantville community on June 5, 1997. Since then, a second hangar has been built to further restore and display vintage aircraft. In 2003, the state of North Carolina designated the Asheboro Municipal Airport as the official location of the North Carolina Aviation Museum and the North Carolina Aviation Hall of Fame.

For Randolph County, the last quarter of the twentieth century was a period of growth in many areas, including its population, economic base, education system, and the arts. Leaders have increasingly emphasized and promoted the advantages of attracting new industries and tourists to the area. Despite economic setbacks in the beginning of the twenty-first century—the closings of several manufacturing plants, and cutbacks and layoffs in others— Randolph County has seen recent improvements. In January 2007, the Randolph County Economic Development Corporation reported a 5 percent unemployment rate and other encouraging economic news from 2006, including announcements of $150 million in new and expanded industrial development and 673 new jobs created. Such news is reminiscent of history: when Randolph County has faced difficulties, residents and county leaders have risen to meet challenges and find solutions. They will undoubtedly continue in that tradition.

Works Consulted

Arnett, Ethel Stephens. *The Saura and Keyauwee in the Land that Became Guilford, Randolph, and Rockingham*. Greensboro, N.C.: Media, 1975.
_____. *William Swaim, Fighting Editor: The Story of O. Henry's Grandfather*. Greensboro, N.C.: Piedmont Press, 1963.
Ashe, Samuel A., Stephen B. Weeks, and Charles L. Van Noppen, eds. *Biographical History of North Carolina from Colonial Times to the Present*. 8 vols. Greensboro, N.C.: Charles L. Van Noppen, 1905-1917.
Auman, Dorothy, and Walter Auman, comps. *Seagrove Area*. Asheboro, N.C.: Village Printing, 1976.
Auman, William T. "Neighbor against Neighbor: The Inner Civil War in the Central Counties of Confederate North Carolina." Ph.D. diss., University of North Carolina at Chapel Hill, 1988.
_____. "Neighbor against Neighbor: The Inner Civil War in the Randolph County Area of Confederate North Carolina." *North Carolina Historical Review* 61 (January 1984): 59-92.
_____. "North Carolina's Inner Civil War: Randolph County." Master's thesis, University of North Carolina at Greensboro, 1978.
Barrett, John G. *The Civil War in North Carolina*. Chapel Hill: The University of North Carolina Press, 1963.
Blair, J. A. *Reminiscences of Randolph County*. Greensboro, N.C.: Reece and Elam, 1890.
Boatner, Mark Mayo III. *The Civil War Dictionary*. New York, N.Y: David McKay Company, 1959.
Branson, Levi. *Branson's North Carolina Business Directory*. 9 vols. Raleigh, N.C.: L. Branson, 1866-1897.
Burgess, Fred. *Randolph County: Economic and Social: A Laboratory Study at the University of North Carolina, Department of Rural Social Economics*. 1924. Reprint, Asheboro, N.C.: Randolph County Historical Society, 1969.
Burgin, Emma. "Pisgah Surveys Damage," *High Point Enterprise*, August 12, 2003, http://www.hpe.com/.
Chaffin, Nora Campbell. *Trinity College, 1839-1892: The Beginnings of Duke University*. Durham, N.C.: Duke University Press, 1950.
City of Greensboro, "Project Updates: Randleman Dam," *City Connections* 6, no.1 (January 22, 2007). http://www.greensboro-nc.gov/connections/archive/070122.htm.

Corbitt, David Leroy. *The Formation of the North Carolina Counties 1663-1943*. Raleigh, N.C.: State Department of Archives and History, 1950.

De Roulhac Hamilton, J. G., ed. *The Correspondence of Jonathan Worth*. 2 vols. Raleigh, N.C.: Edwards and Broughton, 1909.

Fanning, David. *The Narrative of Colonel David Fanning*. 1865. Reprint, Spartanburg, S.C.: Reprint Company, 1973.

Folk, Edgar E., and Bynum Shaw. *W. W. Holden, A Political Biography*. Winston-Salem, N.C.: John F. Blair, 1982.

Gilbert, John, comp. and ed.; text by Grady Jefferys. *Crossties through Carolina: The Story of North Carolina's Early Day Railroads*. Raleigh, N.C.: Helios Press, 1969.

Harrington, Matt. "Unilever to Shut Down Asheboro Manufacturing Operations." *The Business Journal*, November 11, 2005. http://triad.bizjournals.com/triad/stories/2005/11/14/story4.html?page2

Henderson, Archibald. "The Origin of the Regulation in North Carolina." *American Historical Review* 21 (January 1916): 320-332.

Hinshaw, Seth B. *Friends at Holly Spring: Meeting and Community*. Greensboro, N.C.: Friends Historical Society, 1982.

Lawson, John. *Lawson's History of North Carolina*. 2d ed. Richmond, Va.: Garrett and Massie, 1961.

Lefler, Hugh T., and Albert R. Newsome. *North Carolina: The History of a Southern State*. 3d ed. Chapel Hill: University of North Carolina Press, 1973.

Long, Mary Alves. *High Time to Tell It*. Durham, N.C.: Duke University Press, 1950.

McPherson, James M. *Ordeal by Fire: The Civil War and Reconstruction*. 2nd ed. New York: McGraw Hill, 1992.

Martin, Cheryl Lynn, ed. *The Heritage of Randolph County, North Carolina*. Vol. 1. Asheboro, N.C.: Randolph County Heritage Book Committee, 1993.

Miller, Lee. *Roanoke: Solving the Mystery of the Lost Colony*. New York: Arcade Publishing, 2001.

Nowell, Paul. "Rocking like Kennedy," *SouthCoast Today*, March 17, 1996. Available from http:// www.s-t.com/daily/03-96/03-17-96/1rocker.htm. Accessed September 16, 2003.

Powell, William S. *North Carolina through Four Centuries*. Chapel Hill: University of North Carolina Press, 1989.

_____. *The Proprietors of Carolina*. 1963. Reprint, Raleigh, N.C.: State Department of Archives and History, 1968.

Ragan, Sam. "They Struck Sparks and Lit Literary Lanterns." *North Carolina Historical Review* 55 (Spring 1978): 181-188.

Randolph County Economic Development Corporation. *Randolph County Economic Development Corporation.* http://www.rcedc.com/

Randolph County Historical Society and Randolph Arts Guild. *Randolph County, 1779-1979.* Winston-Salem, N.C.: Hunter Publishing, 1980.

Randolph County Public Library. "Randolph County Historical Photo Collection." *The Randolph County Public Library.* http://randolphlibrary.org/historicalphotos.htm

Randolph County Tourism Development Authority. *Visit Randolph County.* http://www.visitrandolphcounty.com/

Rights, Douglas L. *The American Indian in North Carolina.* 2nd ed. Winston-Salem, N.C.: John F. Blair, 1957.

Robins, Sidney Swaim. *Sketches of My Asheboro: Asheboro, N.C., 1880-1910.* Asheboro, N.C.: Randolph Historical Society, 1972.

Sharpe, Bill. *A New Geography of North Carolina.* Vol. 2. Raleigh, N.C.: Sharpe Publishing, 1958.

South Carolina Department of Transportation. *I-73 Environmental Impact Study.* http://www.i73insc.com/

Spencer, Alexander. *Autobiography of Alexander Spencer.* 1908. Reprint, Manteo, N.C.: Outer Banks History Center, 1989.

Starling, Robert B. "The Plank Road Movement in North Carolina." Parts 1 and 2. *North Carolina Historical Review* 16 (January 1939): 1-22; 16 (April 1939): 147-173.

Swaim, Benjamin. *The Man of Business.* 2 vols. New Salem, N.C.: R. J. West, 1835.

Thompson, Holland. *From the Cotton Field to the Cotton Mill: A Study of the Industrial Transition in North Carolina.* New York, N.Y.: The Macmillan Company, 1906.

U.S. Congress. House. *Memorial Addresses on William C. Hammer.* 71st Cong., 3d sess., 1931. Doc. 808.

Vanhuss, Della M. "Randleman, North Carolina 1848-1895: A Study in the Growth of the Cotton Textile Industry." Master's thesis, University of North Carolina at Greensboro, 1986.

Walker, Harriette Hammer. *Busy North Carolina Women.* Asheboro, N.C.: the author, 1931.

Walker, J. D. "2006 a Good Year for Randolph Economically." *Asheboro Courier-Tribune*, January 8, 2007. http://www.courier-tribune.com/articles/2007/01/08/news/en2.txt

Wall, Addison A., ed. *The Randolph Story.* Randleman, N.C.: Randleman Rotary Club, 1976.

Whatley, Lowell McKay, Jr. *The Architectural History of Randolph County North Carolina*. Compiled by Dawn McLaughlin Snotherly. Essays edited by Jerry L. Cross. Asheboro, N.C.: City of Asheboro, County of Randolph, and North Carolina Division of Archives and History, 1985.

Wheeler, John H. *Reminiscences and Memoirs of North Carolina and Eminent North Carolinians*. 1884. Reprint, Baltimore, Md.: Clearfield, 1993.

Zuber, Richard L. *Jonathan Worth: A Biography of a Southern Unionist*. Chapel Hill: University of North Carolina Press, 1965.

Index

A

A&P (supermarkets), 108

Abolition Methodists (Wesleyan), 50, 51

Abram's Creek, 25

Acme Hosiery Mills, 89, 97. *See also*
Acme-McCrary Corporation; Acme-
McCrary Hosiery

Acme-McCrary Corporation, 90, 126.
See also Acme Hosiery Mills; Acme-
McCrary Hosiery

Acme-McCrary Hosiery, 108, 109. *See
also* Acme Hosiery Mills; Acme-
McCrary Corporation;

Adineal, John, 22

Agriculture, 111, 112, 124-126. *See also*
Farming and farms

A. J. Schneierson (clothing), 107

Alamance, Battle of, 15

Alamance Battleground State Historic
Site, 15

Alberta Chair Company, 71

Allen's Fall, 28, 71. *See also* Ramseur

American Classic Motorcycle Museum,
119

American Home Products. *See* Luck's
Incorporated

American Indian in North Carolina, The
(book), 4

American Missionary Association, 69

American (Know-Nothing) Party, 47

American Red Cross, 103-104

American Revolution. *See*
Revolutionary War

Anglican Church, 11

Archdale, John, 70

Archdale: as site of Tomlinson, English,
and Company, 55; Bush Hill
renamed, 38, 70; early development
of, 39; history museum in, 115;
population of (1990 and 2000), 124;
shuttle block plants operating in, 79;
size of, relative to other towns, 124;
tollhouse at, 32. *See also* Bush Hill

Archdale-Trinity News (newspaper), 129

Armfield, Bob, 118

Armfield, W. J., Jr., 84

Arnold, John, 23, 24

Arrow International (medical supplies),
127

Arthur, Gabriel, 3

Artifacts, 3. *See also* Excavations

Asbury, Bishop Francis, 9

Asheboro: as site of Acme Hosiery Mill,
89, Asheboro Academy, 69, Banner
Hosiery, 108, Barnes- Griffin Clinic,
100, Bicentennial Park, 128, Blue
Gem Manufacturing, 107, first Food
Line supermarkets, 109, Klaussner
Furniture Industries, 109, Klopman
Mills, 105, Memorial Hospital, 98,
Miller Hospital, 98, P&P Chair
Company, 97, 99, Plastic Color-
Chips, 109, Randolph County
Health Department, 99, Union
Carbide Corporation, 105; bank
opens in, 83-84; Benjamin Elliot
owns store in, 26; Benjamin Swaim
moves to, 49; Central High School
for African Americans in, 89; churches
established in, 42; Company K staffed
by men from, 91; described by
prominent residents, 74; developed
after Civil War, 70; downtown of,
77; elections in, 72; established as
county seat, 25; Henry Robins serves
as mayor of, 76; importance of,
because of location, 76; incorporation
of, 42; Marmaduke Swaim Robins
joins law practice in, 49; named for
Samuel Ashe, 25; Native American
artifacts found near, 3; *News and
Record* establishes bureau in, 119; Old
Hickory Café in, 94; population of,
112; rail service in, 85; residents of,
who owned Sapona Cotton Mills
shares, 28; resistance to integration in,
114; size of, as compared to
Ramseur, 72; spelled various ways,
25; tollhouses in, 32; William Cicero
Hammer as mayor of, 47

Asheboro Academy (African American), 69

Asheboro Chair Company, 86

Asheboro City Schools, 127

Asheboro Coffin and Casket Company, 90

Asheboro College (previously Asheboro Commercial College), 112

Asheboro Courier (newspaper), 47, 76, 77, 100

Asheboro Furniture Company, 86

Asheboro Graded School, 68. *See also* Asheborough Male Academy

Asheboro Hosiery Mills, 97, 127

Asheboro Kiwanis Club, 95

Asheboro Lumber and Manufacturing, 90

Asheboro Municipal Airport, 17, 115, 119, 132, 138

Asheboro Municipal Golf Course, 101, 120

Asheboro Presbyterian Church, 7, 41, 42, 43, 63, 69

Asheboro Public Library, 129

Asheboro-Randolph Chamber of Commerce, 119

Asheboro Roller Mills, 89

Asheboro Rotary Club, 95, 102

Asheboro Southern Citizen (newspaper), 41

Asheboro's Woman's Club, 95

Asheboro Telephone, 87

Asheborough Female Academy, 36, 37, 68, 129

Asheborough Male Academy, 36. *See also* Asheboro Graded School

Asheboro Veneer Company, 86

Asheboro Wood and Iron Works, 86

Auman, Dorothy Cole, 117, 135

Auman, Frank, Jr., 122

Auman, Walter, 117, 135

Auman Lumber. *See* Seagrove Lumber

Aviation, 111

B

Back Creek Friends Meeting, 11

Balfour, Andrew, 17, 21

Balfour, Elizabeth Dayton, 17

Ballinger, Henry, 6

Bank of Randolph, 83

Banner Hosiery, 108

Baptists, 119. *See also* Churches: Baptist

Barker, Cyrus, 56

Barker, Nathan, 56

Barnes, Dr. Dempsey, 100

Barnes-Griffin Clinic, 100

Barrett, C. A., 112, 113

Barton, John, 7

Battle, William H., 49

Battle of Alamance, 15

Bay Doe (horse), 17

B. B. Walker Company (footwear), 106, 127

Bean, J. W., 81

Bell, Martha McGee, 19, 20, 21. *See also* McGee, Martha

Bell, William, 7, 19, 20, 22, 23

Bell's Meeting, 10

Bell-Welborn Cemetery, 21

Ben Owen Pottery, 136

Bethel Meeting, 42

Bethel Methodist Protestant Church, 64

Bicentennial celebration, 8

Big Bear (supermarkets), 108

Black and Decker (tools), 127

Blair, Hannah, 21

Blair, J. A., 74, 76-77

Bloodworth, Timothy, 14

Blue Bell (clothing), 107

Blue Gem Manufacturing (clothing), 107

Bobbin factory, 79

Bossong, Charles G., 97

Bossong, Joseph C., 97

Bossong Hosiery Mills, 97, 109

Bost Neckwear, 107, 115

Branson's North Carolina Business Directory of 1894, 42, 86

Brashears, Laura, 95

Bridges, covered, 27, 84, 85, 133-134

Brokaw, W. Gould, 76

Brown, Hardy, 42

Brown, Cpl. Jake, 93

Brown, Joseph, 25

Brown, Reuben H., 49

Brown's School, 37. *See also* Trinity College

Brubaker, Harold James, 123
Buffalo Ford, 18
Bulla, A. N., 89
Bulla, Jefferson Davis, 83
Bulla, T. Fletcher, 88
Bulla Grove. *See* St. Luke's United
  Methodist Church
Bunch, Walter A., III, 102
Bunting, Colon, 93
Bunting, Ernest E., 93
Burial mounds. *See* Native Americans
Burns, Capt. A. E., 86
Burns, Capt. John, 17
Burwick, Oscar W., 112
Busbee, Jacques, 96, 116
Busbee, Juliana, 96, 116, 118, 136
Bush Hill, 38, 39, 55, 64, 70, 82. *See
  also* Archdale
Butler, William, 12, 13

C

Caldwell, David, 14
Callicutt, Hugh, 107
Camp Caraway, 119
Camp Mundo Vista, 119
Canby, Gen. E. R. S., 66
Capel, A. W. E., 71
Caraway Creek, 3, 5
Caraway Furniture, 127
Caraway Speedway, 119
Carolina Power and Light Company
  (CP&L), 87
Carolina Pyrophyllite Mining
  Company, 71
Carolina Rocker. *See* P&P Chair
  Company
Carr, Julian S., 70
Carteret, John (Lord Granville), 5-6
Cedar Falls, 6, 84, 108, 110
Cedar Falls Baptist Church, 42
Cedar Falls Bobbin Company, 79
Cedar Falls Covered Bridge, 27
Cedar Falls Manufacturing Company,
  26-27. *See also* Sapona Cotton Mill
Cedar Square Meeting, 42
Census data, 32-33, 73, 83
Central Falls, 79, 105

Central High School, 89, 112
Centre Friends Meeting, 43, 54
Charmeuse (hosiery), 108
Cheek, Waldo, 122
Chriscoe family, 8, 96
Christian Sun (newspaper), 49
Christian Union Church, 42
Churches: African American, 42;
  Baptist, 9, 10, 42, 71; camp meetings
  as forerunners of, 10; Catholic, 124;
  Christian, 42, 71; Lutheran, 11;
  Methodist, 7, 10, 42, 124; Methodist
  Episcopal, 39, 42, 71; Methodist
  Protestant, 42, 64; non-denomina-
  tional worship among, 10;
  Presbyterian, 41, 42, 43, 69; Puritan,
  7; Quaker, 10, 11, 38, 39, 41, 42, 43,
  54, 82; serve as forerunners of public
  libraries, 95. *See also* individual
  church names
City of Asheboro, 127
Civic clubs and organizations, 95
Civilian Conservation Corps, 101
Civil rights movement, 111, 113-114
Civil War: affects educational funding,
  69; exacerbates teacher shortage, 35;
  local conflict and strife over, 58-65;
  mentioned, 43, 48, 49; migration
  after, 65; peace movement during,
  56-57; prompts Quakers to move,
  39; Randolphians serve in, 57;
  Randolph opposes secession prior to,
  53; relics from, 129
Clark, Henry T., 52, 58
Clark, John Washington, 72, 95
Clark, Walter M., 72
Clark, William, 40
Clark, Capt. William, 16
Cloverleaf (ham company), 108
Cochrane, Betsy Lane, 123
Coe, Dr. Joffre, 4
Coffin, Elisha, 72
Coggins, Miss A., 71
Coggins, Elizabeth, 71
Cole family, 8, 96
Cole, George, 8
Cole, Waymon, 118
Cole, William, 8, 22, 23

Coleridge, 118
Cole's Pottery, 118
Collier, John, 23
Collier, Col. John, 22
Colonial (supermarkets), 108
Colonial assembly, 7
Colonial-era political sentiments, 15
Colonial legislature, 11, 12
Color Chip Corporation. *See* Plastic
    Color-Chips
Colton, Simeon, 41, 68
Coltrane, David S., 95
Coltrane's Mill, 7
Columbia. *See* Ramseur
Columbia Manufacturing, 71. *See also*
    Deep River Mills
Commerce, early, 26
Community Newspaper Holdings, 118
Company K, 120th Infantry, Thirtieth
    Old Hickory Division, 91, 92, 93, 94
Company M, Twenty-second
    Regiment, North Carolina Troops,
    129
ConAgra Grocery Products, 127
Concord Township, 36
Confederacy, 53, 54, 55, 59, 60
Confederate Congress, 42, 53, 62
Congressional Reconstruction, 66
Conscription Act of 1862, 57
Cooper Tire and Rubber, 127
Cornwallis, Lord Charles, 18, 19, 20, 21
Cortner, George, 23
County formation, 22
County of Randolph, 127
County seat and courthouse established,
    25. *See also* Courthouse, early;
    Randolph County Courthouse
Courier-Tribune (newspaper), 100, 118,
    129
Courthouse, early, 23. *See also* County
    seat and courthouse established;
    Randolph County Courthouse
Covered bridges. *See* Bridges, covered
Covington, Marion Moring Stedman,
    116
Cox, Harmon, 18
Cox, Isham, 54
Cox, Nathan, 51

Cox, Roy, Sr., 100, 119
Cox, Thomas, 18
Cox's Mill, 18
Cranford, Chisholm C., 89, 97, 105
Cranford, E. H., 86
Craven family, 96
Craven, Braxton: co-publishes *Southern
    Index*, 49; decries South's dependence
    on the North, 51; helps develop
    Trinity College, 36-37; organizes
    Trinity Guard, 58, 59; serves as
    president of Trinity College, 52
Craven, Peter, 8
Croker, J. T., 76
Cultural activities, 111, 115, 116
Cutright, Paul, 118

D

Daniel, Martitia, 44
Dart Container (plastics), 126
Davis, Clarence, 108
Davis, Enoch, 23
Deal, R. P., 90
Deep River: Benjamin Elliott builds
    dam and sawmill on, 26; Bishop
    Francis Asbury crosses, 9; Cedar Falls
    Covered Bridge spans, 27;
    Continental Army camps at, 18; dams
    affect fishing on, 7-8; depicted on
    1733 map, 2; Dicks (Dicks Crossing)
    located on, 39; Herman Husband
    purchases land on, 6; mentioned, 1,
    28; Quakers settle on, 10; William
    Bell builds mill at, 7; William
    Millikan's house on, 17
Deep River Mills, 90. *See also*
    Columbia Manufacturing
De Kalb, Gen. Johann, 18
Dent, William, 22
Dependable Hosiery, 97
Derr, Robert, 118
Dicks, Peter, 39
Dicks, Sarah, 46
Dicks (Dicks Crossing), 28, 39. *See also*
    Randleman
Distilleries, 82
Dixon, Capt. Ben F., 91-93

Dixon, Wright, 91, 92
Dixon Post 45, 94
Donrey Media Group, 118
Dougan, Tom, 23
Drake, James M. A., 42
Duke, Washington, 70
Duke Power, 87
Duke University, 70. *See also* Trinity
   College
Dunkers, 6, 15, 50

E

Elastic Therapy (hosiery), 127
Elison, Sarah Harper, 43
Elliott, Benjamin, 26, 27
Elliott, Henry B., 41
Elliott, Henry Branson (son of
   Benjamin Elliott), 26, 27, 84
Ellis, Tom, 122
Elrod, John, 16
Emigrants, 30
Energizer Battery, 126
English. *See* Tomlinson, English, and
   Company
Ervin, Sam J., Jr., 46
Evergreen (periodical), 49
Excavations, 8, 9

F

Fairway Park, 76
Faith Rock, 17
Fanning, Col. David, 17, 18
Fanning, Edmund, 12, 13
Farmer Academy, 68
Farming and farms, 6, 32, 35, 69, 119
Fenburg, Jerry, 118
Ferree, A. I., 100
Ferree, John H., 40, 71, 90, 98
Ferree, John R., 90
Ferree Memorial Hospital, 98
Field & Dicks Mill, 8
Financial institutions, 83, 84
First United Methodist Church
   (Asheboro Methodist Episcopal
   Church), 42
Fisher, Capt. Basil J., 80, 82

Food Line (supermarkets), 108
Forrester, Sgt. William O., 93
Foust, Mrs. I. H., 61
Foust's Mill, 56
Fox family, 8
Fox, Charlesanna, 36
Franklin, Jesse, 41
Franklinsville, 28. *See also* Franklinville
Franklinville: Andrew Hunter escapes
   at, 17; as site of smeltery, 56; covered
   bridge at, 84; early development of,
   41; Middleton Academy near, 36;
   population of (1880), 72, (1950-
   1970), 112, (1990 and 2000), 124
Franklinville Township, 81
Freedmen's Bureau, 69
Friday Afternoon Book Club, 95
Friends at Holly Spring (book), 54
Frohock, John, 12
From the Cotton Field to the Cotton Mill
   (book), 27, 28
Fuller, E. W., 97
Furniture industry growth, 79

G

Galey and Lord (textiles), 127
Galifianakis, Nick, 122
Gant, Zebulan, 6
Gates, Gen. Horatio, 18
General Electric Company, 106
George Washington Carver College,
   112, 113
Girl Scouts, 95
Gold mining, 80
Gold Star Memorial Board, 102
Gollihorn, Alpheus, 62
Gollihorn, Milton, 62
Gollihorn, William, 62
Gollihorn Spring, 62
Goodyear Tire and Rubber, 127
Grant, Gen. Ulysses S., 64
Grant Township, 56, 120
Grantville, 138
Granville, Lord. *See* Carteret, John
Graves, D. Clyde, 107
Graves, Nell Cole, 118

Gray, Alexander, 43
Gray, Gen. Alexander, 41, 50
Great Alamance Creek, 13
Great Awakening (religious
  movement), 7
Great Depression, 100, 103, 104
Great Trading Path, 2, 5. *See also*
  Native Americans
Great Wagon Road, 8
Greensboro Academy, 43
Greensboro Patriot (newspaper), 47
Gregson Manufacturing (furniture), 97
Grey, Richard. See Richard Grey
  Hosiery
Griffin. *See* Barnes-Griffin Clinic
Griffin, Dr. Harvey Lee, 100
Guilford Battle Chapter, National
  Society of the Daughters of the
  American Revolution, 21
Gwaltney of Smithfield. *See* Hancock's
  Old Fashion Country Ham

H

Hafele America Company (furniture
  hardware), 126
Hamlet, Carl, 107
Hammer, Minnie Hancock, 100
Hammer, William Cicero, 25, 46, 47,
  77, 100
Hammond, Moses, 82
Hancock, Wilbert, 107
Hancock's Old Fashion Country Ham,
  107
Hardin, Myrtle, 110
Hardin's Wholesale Florist, 110
Harper, Jeduthan, 23, 43
Harper, Jesse, 41
Harrelson, Albert A., Jr., 106
Harrelson Rubber Company, 106
Harvey, John, 25
Haworth, Eli, 39
Hayworth, C. A., 98
Hayworth, Ray W., 98
Helms, Jesse, 122
Hendricks, G. G., 89
Henley, Jesse, 25
Henley, Jesse, Jr., 25

Hill, Aaron, 24
Hill, John C., 56
Hinds, John, 22, 23
Hinds, Joseph, 23
Hinshaw, Elizabeth, 56
Hinshaw, Jacob, 56
Hinshaw, Mary, 56, 57
Hinshaw, Seth B., 54
Hinshaw, Thomas, 56, 57
Hodges, Luther, Jr., 122
Hoggett, Anthony, 6
Holden, William Woods, 56, 57, 66
Holland, Dwight M., 115
Holly Spring Meeting, 10, 54
Home Building Materials, 90
Home Guard, 49, 59, 60, 61
Hoover, Andrew, 16. *See also* Huber,
  Andreas
Hoover, Herbert, 16
Hoover, Joseph, 80
Hoover Hill Mine, 80
Hopewell Methodist Episcopal Church,
  39
Horney family, 41
Horney, Alexander S., 26, 27
Horney, Dr. Philip, 26, 27
Hospitals. *See* Medical services
Huber, Andreas, 6, 7. *See also* Hoover,
  Andrew
Huger, Gen. Isaac, 19
Hughes Furniture Industries, 126
Humble Mills (pottery), 118
Hunter, Andrew, 17
Hunter, Mrs. Andrew, 17
Hunter, James, 14, 23
Hunter, T. A., 90
Husband, Herman, 6, 12, 14

I

Indentured white orphans, 33
Indian Trading Path, 2
Industrial development, 28, 138
Industry, 8, 102, 111, 127
Ingram, John Randolph, 122
Iron Mountain, 56
I. Schneierson and Sons (textiles), 107

J

Jackson, Andrew, 24
Jackson, Elvira Worth, 95
Jackson, Herbert Worth, 78
Jackson, Samuel S., 49
Jail. *See* Municipal services
Jennings, A. G., 79
Joe Owens Shop (pottery), 118
Johnson, Andrew, 66, 67
Johnson, T. A., 97
Johnston, Joseph E., 64
Johnston, Samuel, 23
Johnstonville, 23, 24, 25
Jones, Dr. David, 133
Jones, Jerry, 115
Jordan, B. Everett, 111
Jordan, Dr. Henry, 110
Joyner, Dr. George W., 99
JRA Industries (hosiery), 109, 115
Jugtown (land Jacques Busbee purchased and named), 96
Jugtown (previously Busbee's Jugtown Pottery), 118
Jugtown Pottery, 116, 136

K

K & W Cafeteria, 130
Kayser-Roth (textiles), 126
Keeauwee Old Town, 2
Kennedy Rocker. *See* P & P Chair Company
Kivett, Pvt. John, 93
Klaussner, Hans, 109
Klaussner Furniture Industries, 109, 126
Klopman, William, 105
Klopman Industries (textiles), 127
Klopman Mills (textiles), 105-106

L

Lail, Jack, 109
Lambert, Dr. W. L., 98
Lambeth, TSgt. Benjamin F., 102
Lambeth, Mr. and Mrs. T. J., 102
Lance Company. *See* Hancock's Old Fashion Country Ham

Lane, John, 24
Lane, Dr. William B., 83
Laughlin Hosiery Mill, 108
Lawson, John, 3
Leach, I. E., 47
Leach, James Madison, 47, 48
Lederer, John, 2
Lee, Gen. Robert E., 61, 64, 78
Level Cross, 135
Lewis, Jonathan, 73
Liberty: as site of Dependable Hosiery and Gregson Manufacturing, 97; early development in, 41; in early twentieth century, 88; mentioned, 70; population of (1950 to 1970), 112, (1990 and 2000), 124; school for African Americans closed in, 114; sources of electricity for, 87; Southern Railway stops at, 86
Liberty Academy. *See* Normal College
Liberty Antiques Festival, 119
Liberty Chair Company, 87
Liberty Furniture Company, 71
Liberty Herald (newspaper), 119
Liberty News (newspaper), 100, 129
Liberty Picker-Stick and Novelty Company. *See* Liberty Furniture Company
Liberty Register (newspaper), 77, 119
Liberty Rotary Club, 95
Liberty *Villager* (newspaper), 119
Libraries, early, 95
Lincoln, Abraham, 52
Lindley Park School, 114
Lions Club, 95
Liquor laws, 130-131
Literary Fund, 35, 69
Little River, 1, 84, 85
Long, James, 47
Long, John, Jr., 41, 46-47
Long, Dr. John Wesley, 47, 94
Long, William J., 47
Lords Proprietors, 6
Love, Stuart, 109
Lovett, Lt. Clarence J., 91
Lowe, John, 23

Loyalists, 13, 15, 16, 17, 18, 19
Loyal Militia of Randolph and
Chatham counties, 17
Lucas, W. Clyde, 97, 119
Luck family, 8, 96
Luck, Ivey B., 107, 108
Luck's Incorporated (canned food),
107, 108, 127
Lutherans, German, 11. *See also*
Churches: Lutheran

M

Makepeace family, 41
Malaria, 5
Manufacturing, 97, 126. *See also*
individual companies by name
Manufacturing Company of the County
of Randolph. *See* Cedar Falls
Manufacturing Company
Manumission Society, 43, 50, 54
March Furniture Manufacturing, 126
Marie Antoinette Mills, 90
Marietta Masonic Lodge #444, 72
Marlborough Meeting, 11
Marley, Mary, 112
Marsh, Alfred, 42
Martin, Alexander, 14
Martin, J. A., 80
Martin, James, 22
Mary Barker (book), 49
MatLab (plastics and metals), 138
McAlister, Adelaide (nee Worth), 78
McAlister, Alexander Worth, 78
McAlister, Lt. Col. Alexander Cary,
61-62, 78, 86
McAlister, C. C., 90
McAllister. *See* McAlister
McCain, Hugh, 26, 42
McCrary, Charles W., 112
McCrary, Charles Walker, Sr., 99
McCrary, D. B., 89, 99, 111
McCrary Ball Park, 109
McCrary Eagles, 109
McCrary Hosiery Mills, 97
McCulloh, Henry, 6
McCulloh, Henry Eustace, 23

McCullom, Duncan, 6
McDowell, Ira L., 128
McDowell, Thomas J., 93
McGee, Betty, 21
McGee, Col. John, 10
McGee, John, Jr., 10
McGee, Martha, 10. *See also* Bell,
Martha McGee
McGee, William, 10
McLauchlin, Joseph, 71
McMasters, William, 9
McNeill family, 96
Mead, William E., 69
Medical services, 83, 98, 99. *See also*
individual hospitals and physicians by
name
Melanchton Lutheran Church, 11
Memorial Hospital, 80, 82, 98
Mendenhall, Elisha, 7
Merrell, William, 23
Methodist Episcopals. *See* Churches:
Methodist Episcopal
Methodist Protestants, 41. *See also*
Churches: Methodist; Churches:
Methodist Protestant
Methodists, 37. *See also* Churches:
Methodist
Methodist Society, 9
Meyer, Jacob, 9
Middleton Academy, 36, 41
Mid-State Plastics, 109
Migration, 30, 65
Millburg, Larry, 107
Miller, Dr. J. F., 98
Miller, Mrs. J. F., 98
Miller, Lee, 4
Miller Hospital, 98
Millikan, William, 17, 22, 23
Millikan Sausage, 107
Mills, L. Barron, Jr., 118
Mills. *See* individual mills by name
Mills, cotton: close during the Great
Depression, 100; in Ramseur, 87;
mentioned, 26, 50, 72, 73, 81;
produce goods for the Confederacy,
55
Mills, grist, 7, 16, 26, 39, 72

Mills, hosiery: mentioned, 70, 86, 89, 97, 108-109; produce for the military, 103
Mills, lumber, 7, 26
Mills, textile, 40, 71
Millstone Creek, 18
Mines and mining, 2, 71, 80. *See also* individual mines by name
Mines, copper, 81
Mines, gold, 2, 81
M. L. Owens Pottery, 118
Moffitt family, 86
Moffitt, Elvira Worth Jackson Walker, 78
Moffitt, Reverend Thomas C., 42
Moore, Col. William, 23
Moravians, 5, 6, 8, 9, 15, 50
Morehead, John Motley, 29
Morgan, Phil, 118
Moring, W. H., 77
Moring, W. H., Sr., 63
Moring Center. *See* W. H. Moring Jr. Arts Center
Morris, Christian, 72
Moseley, Edward, 2
Moser, D. Wescott, 120
Mountain View Canning Company. *See* Luck's Incorporated
Mount Shepherd, 119
Mr. Jeans (clothing), 107
Muddy Creek, 20
Municipal services, 128
Murphey, Archibald DeBow, 44
Museum of North Carolina Traditional Pottery, 135

N

Naomi Falls, 73
Naomi Falls Manufacturing Company, 90
NASCAR, 119
National Chair Company, 97
Native Americans, 2-4
Needham, John, 3
Neutrals, 15, 17
New Garden meetinghouse, 21

Newlin, S. G., 89
New Market, 32
New Market Township, 20
New Salem, 9, 40, 41, 49, 84
New Salem Masonic Lodge, 41
New Salem Meeting, 41
News and Record (Greensboro), 118
Newspapers, 49, 118-119, 129. *See also* individual newspapers by name
New Voyage to North Carolina, A, (book), 3
Nixon, Phineas, 25
Normal College (previously Brown's School, Union Institute; later Trinity College, Duke University). *See* Trinity College
Normal College (previously Liberty Academy), 70
North Carolina Aviation Hall of Fame, 138
North Carolina Aviation Museum, 119, 132, 138
North Carolina Bulletin (newspaper), 49
North Carolina Historical Exploration group, 8
North Carolina Jaycees, 119
North Carolina Potters Conference, 128
North Carolina Pottery Center, 119, 135, 136
North Carolina Yearly Meeting of Friends, 33
North Carolina Zoological Park and Botanical Gardens, 120, 121, 130, 131, 134
Novelty Wood Works, 80

O

Occaneechi Trail. *See* Great Trading Path
O. Henry. *See* Porter, William Sydney
Old Gap Pottery, 118
Old Hickory Café, 94
Old Hickory Division. *See* Company K
Old Plank Road Pottery, 136
Old Union Methodist, 10
Oliver Rubber, 127

Opposition Party, 48
Owen family, 96
Owen, Avery, 137
Owen, B. Wade, Jr., 136
Owen, Ben, 96, 97, 136
Owen, Ben, III, 136, 137
Owen, LoriAnn Little, 137
Owen, Richardson, 23
Owen, Thomas, 22
Owens family, 8
Owens, Boyd, 118
Owens, Joe. *See* Joe Owens Shop
Owens, M. L. *See* M. L. Owens Pottery
Owens, William, wife of, 61

P

P&P Chair Company, 97, 98, 99, 126
Page family, 62, 85
Page, James, 32, 62
Page, Martha Shamburger, 62
Page, William Carl, 97, 99
Parks Cross Roads Christian Church, 42
Patriots, 16, 20
Peace Party, 57, 66
Peirce, Windsor, 23
Pell family, 118
Petty family, 134
Petty, D. M., 38
Petty, Kyle, 134
Petty, Linda, 135
Petty, Pattie, 134
Petty, Richard, 119, 134, 135
Petty, W. C., 38
Pettycord, Jim, 138
Pettycord, Rick, 138
Pettycord Foundation for Aircraft
    Conservation, 138
Pfautz, Margaret, 16
Phillips, Matilda, 122
Phillips Brothers (ham company), 108
Physicians. *See* Medical services
Piedmont Land Conservancy, 134
Piedmont Triad Regional Water
    Authority (PTRWA), 131, 132
Pike, Col. Alfred, 61
Pinehurst Textiles, 107

Pinewood Country Club, 109
Pisgah Covered Bridge, 84, 85, 133-134
Plaidville Mills, 90
Plank roads, 30, 31, 32, 46, 62
Plastic Color-Chips (plastics), 109
Pleasant Grove Christian Church, 42
Pleasant Ridge Christian Church, 42
Plunket, William, 23
Polecat Creek, 6
Political Broadaxe (newspaper), 119
Pollet, Phillip, 118
Population: at county's formation, 23;
    in 1780, 33; in 1860, 50; in 1900, 87;
    in 1950, 111; in 1970, 112; in 1980
    to 2000, 124; per board of education
    statistics, 88; various cities', 112, 124
Porter, Ruth Worth, 78
Porter, William Sydney, 78
Potter, A. D., 107
Potter, A. J., 107
Potter Manufacturing Company
    (clothing), 107, 115
Potters, other livelihoods of, 9. *See also*
    individual potteries (studios) and
    potters by name
Pottery: growth of, during 1950s-
    1970s, 111; museums, 135-136;
    revival of, after World War I, 96;
    revival of, in late twentieth century,
    116-118
Presidential Reconstruction, 66
Presnell, Arthur, 97, 99
Presnell, Clay, 107
Presnell, Teak, 115
Prestige Fabricators (foam products), 127
Prohibition Party, 82
Protestants, German-speaking, 6
Providence Friends Meeting Cemetery,
    73
Providence Meeting, 10
Public libraries, 95
Public schools, 88. *See also* Schools
Pugh, Hal, 9
Pugh, James, 14, 15
Pugh, Phil, 118
Purgatory Mountain, 120

Q

Quakers: as potters, 8, 9; Baltimore Friends establish a model farm for, 70; congregations of, in late 1900s, 124; discourage purchase and separation of slaves, 33-34; employed at saltworks near Wilmington, 55; forcibly conscripted, 56; from Guilford County, 38; in New Salem, 40; mentioned, 28, 69; migration of, 50, 56, 65: move to Piedmont beginning in 1740s, 10-11; of Bush Hill, 38-39; opposed to bearing arms, 53, Civil War, 56, slavery, 50; resist participation in Revolutionary War, 15-16; support Underground Railroad, 54; work with Methodists to develop Union Institute, 37

R

Radio stations, early, 119
Railroad(s): Aberdeen and Asheboro (A & A), 74, 85, 86, 117; Aberdeen and West End, 85; Asheboro and Montgomery (A & M), 85; Atlantic and North Carolina, 46: Cape Fear and Yadkin Valley, 29, 70, 71; change Asheboro's business district, 86; first, in state, 29; General Assembly begins chartering and funding for, 29; High Point, Randleman, Asheboro, and Southern (HPRA & Southern), 85, 86; investors sought for, 41; nearest Randolph by 1860, 29; North Carolina, 30
Rains, Capt. George, 18
Rains, Maj. John, 18
Raleigh Conservative (newspaper), 49
Rampon Products (hosiery), 109, 115
Ramsay, J. M., Jr., 109
Ramseur, Maj. Gen. Stephen D., 71
Ramseur: as site of Novelty Wood Works, 80; Cape Fear and Yadkin Valley Railway builds spur line to, 71; CCC camp near, 101; development of, 71-72; earlier names for, 28, 71; Lions Club of, 95; population of (1950 to 1970), 112 (1990 and 2000), 124; power plant built for cotton mill in, 87
Ramseur Baptist Church, 42
Ramseur Broom Company, 71
Ramseur Bulletin (newspaper), 118
Ramtex (textiles), 126
Randleman, John Banner, 40
Randleman: as site of Randleman Hosiery Mill, 89, Ferree Memorial Hospital, 98, Mr. Jeans, 107, Randolph Underwear Company, 107, United Brass Works, 106; early development of, 39; early sources of electricity for, 87; hard hit by Great Depression, 100; history museum in, 115; Lions Club of, 95; New Salem Masonic Lodge moves to, 41; population of (1950 to 1970), 112, (1990 and 2000), 124; size of, as compared to Ramseur, 72. *See also* Randleman Mills
Randleman Blazer (newspaper), 119
Randleman Chair Company, 90
Randleman Dam. *See* Randleman Lake
Randleman High School (mentioned), 131
Randleman Hosiery Mill, 89
Randleman Lake, 131, 132
Randleman Manufacturing Company (textiles), 40, 90. *See also* Union Factory
Randleman Mills, 73. *See also* Randleman
Randleman News (newspaper), 119
Randleman Reporter (newspaper), 118
Randleman Telephone, 87
Rand Ol' Opry (music hall), 119
Randolph, Peyton, 22
Randolph Argus (newspaper), 77
Randolph Arts Guild, 116. *See also* RSVP Community Theatre
Randolph Chair Company, 89

Randolph Community College, 105, 114, 115, 126

Randolph County Courthouse, 41, 75, 86, 101, 128, 129. *See also* County seat and courthouse established; Courthouse, early

Randolph County Economic Development Corporation, 138

Randolph County Health Department, 99

Randolph County Historical Society, 129

Randolph County Schools, 127

Randolph County, 1779-1979 (book), 36

Randolph County Society for Zoological Development, 120

Randolph County Training School. *See* Central High School

Randolph Electric Membership, 87

Randolph Fall Festival, 115, 116

Randolph Guide (newspaper), 118, 129

Randolph Herald (newspaper), 49

Randolph Hornets, 129

Randolph Hospital, 99, 127, 129

Randolphian (newspaper), 119

Randolph Industrial Education Center. *See* Randolph Community College

Randolph Packing Company, 107

Randolph Power Company, 87

Randolph Regulator (newspaper). See *Asheboro Courier*

Randolph Sun (newspaper), 76

Randolph Technical Institute. *See* Randolph Community College

Randolph Telephone Membership Corporation, 88

Randolph Tourist Development Bureau, 119

Randolph Tribune (newspaper), 100

Randolph Underwear Company. *See* A. J. Schneierson

Ransower, Henry, 25

Rationing, 94, 103, 104

Red Cross (community), 64

Redding, John F., 107

Redding, T. H., 89

Reece, Abraham, 22, 23

Regulators, 12, 13, 14, 15

Religious groups (mid-eighteenth century), 9

Reminiscences of Randolph County (book), 73

Revolutionary War, 7, 16, 18, 22

Reynolds, Jeremiah, 6

Richard Grey Hosiery, 108, 115

Richard Petty Museum, 119

Richardson, Sgt. Hal E., 93

Richland Creek Herb and Flower Farm, 119

Richland Lutheran Church, 11

Richland Township, 72

Rich's on Caraway, 5

Ridges Mountain, 134

Rigdon, Stephen, 23

Rights, Dr. Douglas, 4

Roanoke: Solving the Mystery of the Lost Colony (book), 4

Robbins, William McKendree, 47

Robins, Annie Eliza Moring, 76, 77

Robins, Henry Moring, 76, 130

Robins, Marmaduke Swaim, 48, 76, 129-130

Robins, Sidney Swaim, 74, 76

Roosevelt, Franklin D., 76

Ross, Arthur, 90, 97

Ross, Charles, 111

Ross, Esther, 90

Ross, J. D., 90

Ross, L. Ferree, 90

RSVP Community Theatre, 128. *See also* Randolph Arts Guild

Rush, Wiley, 77

S

Salem, 118

Salem Neckwear, 107

Sandy Creek, 6, 7, 19

Sandy Creek Baptist Church, 9, 10

Sapona Cotton Mill, 28, 103. *See also* Cedar Falls Manufacturing Company

Sapona Manufacturing Company (hosiery), 108
Schneirson, A. J., 107
Schools: Baltimore Association of Friends maintain, 69; desegregation of, 112-114; development of public, after Civil War, 68-70; early private, 36-37; early public, 34-35; early teacher shortages at, 35; for African Americans, 69, 112; integration of, 111; options prior to establishment of public, 34. *See also* individual schools by name
Science Hill (school), 36
Seagrove: as only incorporated town in southern Randolph, 124; coopers in, 82; early development in, 74, 76; early potters in, 8; location of, 8; population of (1950 to 1970), 112, (1990 and 2000), 124; potters in (1976), 118; pottery industry in (1915), 96, (2001), 135; tradition of pottery in, 136; train depot in, 135-136
Seagrove Lumber, 76
Seagrove Potters Museum, 117
Seagrove Pottery Festival, 135
Seagrove School (mentioned), 135
Seagroves, Edwin G., 74
Sealy (mattresses), 127
Settlers: early, 4, 5, 6; German, 9, 11, 15
Shady Grove Baptist Church, 42
Shepherd Mountain, 2, 8, 9
Shepherd Mountain Retreat Center, 8
Sheppard, Jacob, 22, 23
Sheriff's department. *See* Municipal services
Sherman, William T., 61, 63
Sherman's Carolinas Campaign, 63, 64
Shiloh Academy, 68
Shiloh Christian Church, 42
Shuttle block plants, 79
Simmons, Abraham, 33
Sketches of My Asheboro: Asheboro, North Carolina, 1880-1910 (book), 74
Slavery: debate over, less important to Randolph, 50: opposition to, 16, 32, 43, 50; perceived threats to, 46;

Quakers accused of fostering, 51; referendum to abolish, 34. *See also* Slaves
Slaves: few, in area during early settlement, 6; freed by Thirteenth Amendment, 66; leave county, 69; low rates of ownership of, affect support for Confederacy, 52-53; owned by Alexander Gray, 43; owners of, exempted from conscription, 54; population of (1780 to 1860), 50; small number of, before 1850, 28; supervised by Martha Page, 62; used by railroad companies, 29. *See also* Slavery
Smallpox, 4
Smith, C. C., 107
Smitherman, Noah, 34
Snow, Capt. William H., 79
Snow Lumber, 79
Sorosis Club, 95
Southern Christian Church, 49
Southern Citizen (newspaper), 49, 83
Southern Crown Milling Company, 89
Southern Index (periodical). See *Evergreen*
Spangenberg, Bishop August Gottlieb, 5
Spanish influenza pandemic, 94, 98
Spencer, Alexander, 33
Spencer, Alfred, 107
Spencer, J. S., 71
Spencer, L. A., 89
Springfield, 69
Springfield Meeting, 38, 39, 42, 82
Staley, Col. John W., 71
Staley, 71, 112, 124
Staley Cotton Mill, 71
Staley Hosiery Mill, 71, 97
Staleyville. *See* Staley
Star (Montgomery County), 85
StarPet, 127
State constitutional convention, 46
Stearns, Reverend Shubal, 9, 10
Stedman, Sulon B., 103, 106
Stedman, W. David, 106, 120
Stedman Bobbin Factory, 86
Stedman Corporation, 128
Stedman Manufacturing Company (clothing), 103, 106

Steeds (town), 118
Still, Samuel, 16
Stinking Quarter Creek, 7
St. Joseph's Catholic Church, 124
St. Luke's United Methodist Church
   (Bulla Grove), 42
Stoneman, George, 62, 63
Stoneman's Raiders, 62
Story of Naomi Wise, The, or, The
   Wrongs of a Beautiful Girl (book), 49
Stuart Furniture Industries, 109
Sumner, Dr. George H., 98, 99
Swaim, Benjamin, 40-41, 49
Sweezy, Hobert, 118
Sweezy, Nancy, 118

T

Tabernacle Township, 8, 56, 80, 81
Tatom, Absalom, 22
Taxes, 7, 12, 23, 33, 69
Teague, Duck, 118
Technimark (plastics), 126
Temperance movement, 82
Thirtieth Division. See Company K
Thomas Brothers (ham company), 108
Thompson, Holland, 27, 28
Tie-Rite, 107
Timken Company, The (roller
   bearings), 127
Tippett, J. W., 79
Tip-Top Hosiery Mills, 97
Tomlinson, Allen U., 38, 42
Tomlinson, Josiah, 39
Tomlinson, William, 39
Tomlinson, English, and Company
   (tannery), 38, 55
Tories. See Loyalists
Totero Fort, 2
Tourism, 119
Trade (mid-1700s), 8
Transportation: early improvements in,
   29-32; first graded and paved roads as
   form of, 95; highway construction
   for, 130; improvements in (late
   1800s), 84, 85. See also Plank roads;
   Railroads
Trinity, 39, 70, 124

Trinity College: as site of lectures and
   debates, 51; mentioned, 52; moves to
   Durham, 70; opens, 39; prior names
   of, 37; Trinity Guard organized at,
   58; William Robbins is professor of
   mathematics at, 47
Trinity Guard, 58-59
Trinity Township, 23, 37, 50
Trinity Unity School, 113
Trogdon, Ethel Hendrix, 102
Trogdon, Floyd Harrison, 102
Trogdon, Samuel, 25
Trogdon, William H., 102
Tryon, Gov. William, 12, 13

U

UltraCraft (cabinets), 127
Unemployment rate (2006), 138
Unilever, 127
Union (community), 40
Union Carbide Corporation (batteries),
   105
Union Factory (textiles), 39-40. See also
   Randleman Manufacturing Company
Union Institute, 37. See also Trinity
   College
Unionists, 51, 52, 54, 59, 60, 65
Union Manufacturing Company
   (textiles), 28, 40
Union Township, 85
United Brass Works, 106
United Furniture, 126
United Methodist Church, The, 42,
   124. See also Abolition Methodists;
   Churches: Methodist, Methodist
   Episcopal, Methodist Protestant;
   Methodists; Methodist Episcopals;
   Methodist Protestants
U.S. Industries (clothing), 107
Uwharrie Meeting, 11
Uwharrie Mountains, 2, 3, 134
Uwharrie National Forest, 1
Uwharrie (Uhwarre, Heighwarree)
   River, 1, 2, 3, 6, 7, 16

V

Vance, Gov. Zebulon, 49, 53, 57, 61, 66
Vanderford, John, 62
Vernon, Charlie (Braxton Craven pseudonym), 49
Victory Junction Gang Camp, 134-135
Voters and voting, 111, 121-123, 124
Vuncannon Hosiery, 108

W

Wachovia, 5, 6
Wages, manufacturing (2007), 126
Wainman, C. Slingsley, 80
Walker, Al, 108
Walker, Bartlette Burkhead, 106. See also B. B. Walker Company
Walker, Jesse, 26, 31
Walker, Russell, 108
Walker, Russell Grady, 122
Walker, Samuel, 7, 20
Walker's Mill, 20
Wal-Mart, 127
Walters, Pvt. William F., 62
Ward, Earlene Vestal, 112
Ward, W. A., 79
Ward, Wiley, 100
War of the Regulation. See Regulators
Watkins, J. C., 90
Watkins, W. H., 71, 87
Weeks, Dr. Stephen B., 39
Welborn. See Bell-Welborn Cemetery
Welborn Chapel (Baptist church), 42
Welch, J. J., 84
Wells Hosiery, 126
Wesleyans. See Abolition Methodists
Wheeler, Col. John Hill, 45
Whigs, 15, 16, 17, 46
Whiskey. See Distilleries
Whiskey Rebellion, 14
White, J. Logan, 122
W. H. Moring Jr. Arts Center, 116
Why Not Academy, 68

Wiley, Calvin H., 68
Wilkerson, Dr. Charles E., 98-99
Wilkerson, Lula Phillips, 98-99
Winn, Charles St. George, 80
Wise, Naomi, 73
Womack Publishing Company, 118
Wood, Abraham, 3
Wood, Lillie Pearl, 99
Wood, Reuben, 46
Wood, William Penn, 77
Wood, Zebedee, 24, 46
World War I, 91-94
World War II, 101, 102, 103, 104
Worth, Adelaide. See McAlister, Adelaide
Worth, Daniel, 50-51
Worth, Dr. David, 43
Worth, Dr. John Milton: as state treasurer, 48; as superintendent of Wilmington saltworks, 55; business ventures of, 46; marries outside of unity of Friends, 43; mentioned, 78; serves as bank president, 84; serves in state senate, 46; supports amnesty for deserters and conscripts, 61
Worth, Eunice Gardner, 43
Worth, Jonathan: appointed Asheboro commissioner, 42; appointed county school superintendent, 35; attends Greensboro Academy, 43; birth of, 43; business ventures of, 26, 46; children of, 44-45; death and burial of, in Raleigh, 67; denounces nullification, 45-46; early career of, 44-45; elected governor, 44-45; extended family of, 78; helps organize Asheborough Female Academy, 36; moves to Asheboro, 44; pictured, 44; pledges support for Confederacy, 53; runs for governor, 66-67; seeks investors for proposed railroad, 41; serves as state treasurer, 53, 66; views of, on Lincoln's actions, 52
Worth, Joseph Addison, 43, 78

Worth, Laura Stimson, 101
Worth, Martitia, 45
W. P. Wood Company (general
  merchandise), 77

Y

Yates Country Hams, 108
York, Brantley, 37

York, Gordon H., 115
Yow's Mill, 72

Z

Zoo. *See* North Carolina Zoological
  Park and Botanical Gardens